T0318843

Elements in Perception
edited by
James T. Enns
The University of British Columbia

Special Editor for Attention
Marvin Chun
Yale College

COMPETITION AND CONTROL DURING WORKING MEMORY

Anastasia Kiyonaga
University of California, San Diego

Mark D'Esposito
University of California, Berkley

CAMBRIDGE
UNIVERSITY PRESS

University Printing House, Cambridge CB2 8BS, United Kingdom

One Liberty Plaza, 20th Floor, New York, NY 10006, USA

477 Williamstown Road, Port Melbourne, VIC 3207, Australia

314–321, 3rd Floor, Plot 3, Splendor Forum, Jasola District Centre, New Delhi – 110025, India

79 Anson Road, #06–04/06, Singapore 079906

Cambridge University Press is part of the University of Cambridge.

It furthers the University's mission by disseminating knowledge in the pursuit of education, learning, and research at the highest international levels of excellence.

www.cambridge.org
Information on this title: www.cambridge.org/9781108706445
DOI: 10.1017/9781108581073

© Anastasia Kiyonaga and Mark D'Esposito 2020

First published 2020

A catalogue record for this publication is available from the British Library.

ISBN 978-1-108-70644-5 Paperback
ISSN 2515-0502 (online)
ISSN 2515-0499 (print)

Cambridge University Press has no responsibility for the persistence or accuracy of URLs for external or third-party internet websites referred to in this publication and does not guarantee that any content on such websites is, or will remain, accurate or appropriate.

Competition and Control during Working Memory

Elements in Perception

DOI: 10.1017/9781108581073
First published online: October 2020

Anastasia Kiyonaga
University of California, San Diego

Mark D'Esposito
University of California, Berkley

Author for correspondence: Anastasia Kiyonaga, akiyonaga@ucsd.edu

Abstract: Working memory and perceptual attention are related functions, engaging many similar mechanisms and brain regions. As a consequence, behavioral and neural measures often reveal competition between working memory and attention demands. Yet widespread debate remains about how working memory operates, and whether it truly shares processes and representations with attention. This Element will examine local-level representational properties to illuminate the storage format of working memory content, as well as systems-level and brain network communication properties to illuminate the attentional processes that control working memory. The Element will integrate both cognitive and neuroscientific accounts, describing shared substrates for working memory and perceptual attention, in a multilevel network architecture that provides robustness to disruptions and allows flexible attentional control in line with goals.

Keywords: attention, cognitive control, sensory recruitment, visual short-term memory, working memory

ISBNs: 9781108706445 (PB), 9781108581073 (OC)
ISSNs: 2515–0502 (online), ISSN 2515–0499 (print)

Contents

1 Introduction

As humans, we often need to keep several thoughts and goals in mind while we also face immediate demands in our external environment. In other words, we need to "maintain" pertinent information with working memory while we are busy doing (and remembering) other things. We know from everyday experience that this can be difficult. Imagine rehearsing an unfamiliar phone number, which becomes virtually impossible when interrupted by a few moments of conversation or, worse, a stream of numbers on the radio. However, we can also successfully juggle our internal maintenance and external demands in many circumstances. For instance, we can remind ourselves of a shopping list while operating a car and navigating traffic. These conflicting observations, of either fragile or robust working memory, fuel an ongoing debate about whether working memory and (externally oriented) attention overlap in their structure and function. This Element will address this debate by examining when and why internal working memory maintenance competes with externally oriented attention, as well as how goal-directed control processes and whole-brain network reconfiguration can reduce that competition.

Many of the terms that will be used in this Element can take on several meanings, and they often encompass multiple concepts, abilities, or processes. For instance, "attention" refers to something that can be oriented toward its subject, sustained across time, or serve as a filter for what information gets processed. It can operate over locations, objects, or features and be driven by internal goals or environmental cues. Yet across all of these functions, a fundamental property of attention is that it is capacity limited. As a result, attention must be selective. Accordingly, the term "attention" will be used here to mean the selective focusing on a subset of information for further processing. This is achieved by modulation of the neural activity associated with the information being processed, often in a goal-oriented – or "top-down" – manner. That is, perception of a stimulus in the outside world results in a neural response pattern in sensory cortex that depicts the stimulus, and we refer to this depiction as a sensory "representation." When attention is focused on a particular external stimulus, its associated sensory representation is enhanced. Thus, perception activates sensory representations, and those representations are modulated by attention. Here, the term "perceptual attention" will be used to describe attention directed toward external stimuli that are currently present in the environment.

Attention can also be focused internally to maintain representations of recently perceived stimuli or to endogenously activate long-term memory representations for use in the short term. Here, the term "working memory maintenance" will be used to describe attention that is directed internally to modulate representations of information that is unavailable to the senses. Working memory (WM) retains temporary representations that serve many purposes. For instance, representations of the recent sensory past may bridge moments of experience, while more abstract goals may guide behavior throughout an episode. Like "attention," the term "working memory" is often loosely applied and can be used alternatingly to mean a system for short-term retention, a process of short-term maintenance, or a storage location for temporary representations. WM operates across the sensory modalities (verbal, visual, etc.) and wide ranges of task manipulations are used as tests of WM. These tasks place variable demands on processes such as perceptual encoding of the information to be remembered, updating or manipulation of the internal representations, binding of item features, resolution of interference from distractions or disruptions, as well as memory retrieval and decision making at the time when memory is probed. These many cognitive processes can likewise engage distinct neural processes, which rely on varied brain regions and networks. This variability likely contributes to ongoing debates about how WM operates and how WM information is stored. Here, "WM" will refer to the attentional process of maintenance, and the maintained representations that are stored with WM will be referred to as "WM content." This content can span a range including (but not limited to) low-level stimulus features, abstract categorical information, and complex task rules.

Finally, while goal-oriented perceptual attention and WM maintenance are both achieved by top-down modulation of relevant representations, that modulatory process can face competition from additional demands. For instance, visual perceptual attention can be taxed by irrelevant interfering stimuli in the visual field, and WM maintenance can be taxed by a requirement to perform some operation on the WM content. Moreover, perceptual attention can be taxed by concurrent WM maintenance demands, and vice versa. When there is competition among content (e.g., several stimuli to attend) or processes (e.g., internal maintenance vs. external selection), attentional control must be engaged to reduce the competition. That is, there can be local-level competition for stimulus representation as well as systems-level competition among task processes. Here we will use the umbrella term "attentional control" to describe the processes that regulate this competition. That is, while perceptual attention and WM maintenance are themselves modulatory processes that guide ongoing behavior, here we will use "attentional control" to describe the additional modulatory processes that prioritize and apply goal-relevant representations in the face of competition.

This Element will examine local-level properties of WM content to illuminate the storage format of WM, as well as systems-level properties of WM maintenance to illuminate the attentional processes underlying WM. In the first half of the Element, we will address two related issues about the nature of WM: (1) whether WM maintenance activates the same sensory representations as perceptual attention (i.e., whether WM content is "stored" in sensory cortices) and (2) whether WM maintenance and perceptual attention are analogous processes that are achieved via the same neural mechanisms. A central argument against the perspective that WM and perceptual attention share representations and mechanisms is that WM performance is often unimpaired by concurrent perceptual attentional demands (and vice versa). We will first describe evidence for a gradient of competition between WM and perceptual representations that resembles established competitive effects in perceptual attention. This gradient should only exist if WM and perception activate overlapping representations. We will also examine how WM maintenance and perceptual attention can be modulated to limit competition between them, clarifying how these cognitive processes might not always compete (despite activating shared representations). In the second half of the Element, we will examine the brain-wide processes underlying WM maintenance as well as the attentional control processes that are engaged when maintenance is taxed. There is currently widespread debate about the storage substrates and processes that support working memory. Yet the research that sustains this debate has tended to focus on isolated brain regions or maintenance mechanisms, rather than integrating across the brain and across levels of analysis. Therefore, the second half of the Element will address the functional roles of the many brain regions beyond sensory cortex that are involved in WM maintenance, and how those relate to sensory WM representations. We will integrate both cognitive and neuroscientific accounts to propose a multi-level network architecture of WM and perceptual attention that provides robustness to competition and allows flexible attentional control in line with goals.

2 Competition Reveals Mechanisms of WM Storage and Processing

There is now broad agreement that WM and perceptual attention are related functions, engaging many similar mechanisms and brain regions (Awh & Jonides, 2001; Chun, 2011; Chun & Johnson, 2011; Gazzaley & Nobre, 2012; Theeuwes, Kramer, & Irwin, 2011). However, whether WM and perceptual attention truly operate by the same processes and representational substrates is still under debate (Bae & Luck, 2018; Harrison & Bays, 2018; Hollingworth &

Maxcey-Richard, 2012; Leavitt, Mendoza-Halliday, & Martinez-Trujillo, 2017; Mendoza-Halliday & Martinez-Trujillo, 2017; Myers, Stokes, & Nobre, 2017; Nee & Jonides, 2009; van Kerkoerle, Self, & Roelfsema, 2017; Woodman & Luck, 2010; Xu, 2017). For instance, one perspective on WM storage proposes that representations of the remembered content are maintained in prefrontal and parietal brain regions (Leavitt et al., 2017; Xu, 2017), while another proposes dedicated storage "buffers" that are specific to the type of content that is being maintained (e.g., Baddeley & Hitch, 2018; Yue, Martin, Hamilton, & Rose, 2019). These perspectives share the proposal that WM information is represented separately from perceptual stimuli. A clear advantage of such an organization is that it would protect WM content from interference by incoming perceptual input. However, another prominent view asserts that WM activates the same sensory cortical representations as perception (D'Esposito & Postle, 2015; Lara & Wallis, 2015; Pasternak & Greenlee, 2005; Postle, 2006; Serences, 2016; Sreenivasan, Curtis, & D'Esposito, 2014). This framework is appealing in its efficiency, as the same cortical territory can be multipurposed for several kinds of processing, but the theory must reconcile how WM withstands simultaneous perceptual input. The debate between these perspectives can be informed by examining how interactions within and between WM and perceptual content influence behavioral and neural responses. The following sections will therefore examine two hypotheses: (1) If WM activates sensory representations for storage, then perceptual input should influence WM content (and task performance) proportional to the degree of cortical overlap between representations and (2) if WM maintenance operates by the same top-down modulation processes as perceptual attention, then it should be associated with comparable patterns of behavior and be taxed by concurrent perceptual attentional demands.

2.1 WM Maintenance and Perceptual Attention Share Representations

2.1.1 Perceptual Input Influences WM Maintenance

Perceptual attention is limited by the amount and nature of information that it must process. With greater numbers of items and greater similarity between items (e.g., in either location or stimulus features), both behavioral performance and neural response patterns associated with individual items are degraded (Desimone & Duncan, 1995; Pelli & Tillman, 2008; Reddy, Kanwisher, & VanRullen, 2009). That is, items that are represented closer to each other in cortical space are more likely to produce competing neural representations and therefore inhibit each other behaviorally (Franconeri, Alvarez, & Cavanagh, 2013). Consequently, the number of spatial locations that can be attentionally selected is increased when the separation between target locations is increased (Franconeri, Jonathan, & Scimeca, 2010). If WM maintenance and perceptual attention engage the same cortical substrate, WM content and perceptual content should also compete, and in the same manner as perceived stimuli. That is, there should be increased competition between WM and perceptual representations when there is greater overlap between the features of the WM and perceptual content. We can therefore learn about the structure of WM representations by examining how WM performance is influenced by concurrent perceptual input, as described throughout this section.

At the broadest level, when two WM tasks are interleaved, concurrent WM content from the same sensory modality – also sometimes referred to as the WM "domain" – impairs performance more than when the two tasks require memory of content from different modalities. For instance, during verbal WM maintenance for a string of letters or words, a concurrent verbal WM task is more disruptive to performance than a visual WM task (Baddeley, 2003). Although this empirical finding has historically been interpreted as evidence for domain-specific WM storage buffers (e.g., the phonological loop or visuo-spatial sketchpad), it is equally compatible with a revised model of WM storage wherein there is less competition between WM content from different sensory modalities because those representations overlap less in sensory cortex. If perceptual input (rather than concurrent WM demand) were to produce a similar pattern of interference with WM maintenance, it would provide compelling evidence that WM and perceptual content activate shared representations (i.e., interference occurs in sensory cortices rather than dedicated WM buffers).

In keeping with this hypothesis, WM performance is in fact slower and less accurate when distractors presented during WM maintenance are from the same category as the WM content (as opposed to a different category). For instance, during WM delayed recognition for images of faces – when participants were asked to remember a set of images and determine whether a test image matched any items from the WM sample set – performance was impaired more by distractor images of other faces during the WM delay than by images from different categories (e.g., scenes or shoes; Jha & Kiyonaga, 2010; Sreenivasan & Jha, 2007; Yoon, Curtis, & D'Esposito, 2006). Moreover, when WM for faces is tested with continuous recall (rather than recognition), WM recall precision is biased to be more similar to distractor faces that were shown during the delay (Mallett, Mummaneni, & Lewis-Peacock, 2020). Low-level stimuli that vary on a continuous dimension (e.g., orientations or directions of motion) also display a similar gradient of distractor influence, demonstrating that competition between representations of WM content and perceptual input occurs at both the category and exemplar levels, for complex objects as well simple visual features (Magnussen & Greenlee, 1992; Magnussen, Greenlee, Asplund, & Dyrnes, 1991; Nemes, Parry, Whitaker, & McKeefry, 2012; Pasternak & Greenlee, 2005; Rademaker, Bloem, De Weerd, & Sack, 2015; Teng & Kravitz, 2019).

Neural response patterns are also sensitive to the relationship between WM content and perceptual input, illuminating the source of the competition that manifests in behavior. For instance, WM maintenance activity is observed with functional magnetic resonance imaging (fMRI) in the same cortical regions that respond to perception of stimuli from the WM category (Druzgal & D'Esposito, 2001; Ranganath, DeGutis, & D'Esposito, 2004). This finding provides rudimentary evidence that WM storage recruits sensory representations. That interpretation is further corroborated by observations that sensory cortical activity is modulated by the similarity between perceptual input and concurrent WM content. For instance, when a series of faces is presented for comparison to a face item that is being maintained with WM, activity amplitude in face-processing visual regions increases with increasing feature similarity between the WM content and the perceptual input (Sreenivasan, Gratton, Vytlacil, & D'Esposito, 2014). This suggests that WM maintenance may be achieved by feedback signals to perceptual processing and representation regions, which thereby modulate sensory cortical responses to perceptual input. Consistent with this proposed feedback maintenance mechanism, WM for face stimuli is associated with correlated fMRI activity (i.e., functional connectivity) between the lateral prefrontal cortex (PFC) and face-responsive visual regions, suggesting that information is maintained in WM by coactivation between PFC and sensory regions. In other words, lateral PFC may exert top-down modulatory signals that bias or tune sensory representations for WM maintenance.

Maintenance-related coactivation between PFC and face-processing regions is also disrupted by face (but not scene) distractor stimuli, suggesting that this maintenance signal is affected by perceptual input, but only when it competes with the WM content (Postle, Druzgal, & D'Esposito, 2003; Yoon et al., 2006). However, this disruption of presumed communication between PFC and sensory regions during distraction may serve an adaptive purpose – to protect WM from interfering content. For instance, if WM modulation of sensory regions promotes increased responsivity to similar perceptual input (which can impede WM representations), then it would be beneficial to dampen this activity to limit processing of potentially interfering input. Consistent with that interpretation, when distractor face images are presented during a WM maintenance delay period, the face-sensitive N170 event-related potential (ERP) response to those faces is reduced when WM is also for face stimuli (as compared to a different WM category; Sreenivasan & Jha, 2007). This suggests that attentional processing of interfering distractors may be reduced to curtail their impact on WM. Therefore, task-relevant perceptual input can enhance neural signals associated with WM maintenance, while task-irrelevant and detrimental input can disrupt those signals, and both of these modulating effects depend on the degree of similarity between WM and perceptual content.

Going further, multivariate neuroimaging analysis techniques have recently been developed to gauge the pattern of population responses across a set of measurements. These stand in comparison to analysis methods that gauge the mean response amplitude of a region. For instance, for multivariate analyses, electroencephalogram (EEG) data can be analyzed according to the pattern of responses across multiple scalp electrodes, or fMRI data can be analyzed according to the pattern of activity across a selection of voxels (i.e., cubes, or volumetric pixels, that are the MRI unit of measurement in three-dimensional brain space). Machine-learning methods have been applied to such locally distributed patterns of neural activity to either classify (i.e., decode) or reconstruct stimulus representations across a population (Norman, Polyn, Detre, & Haxby, 2006; Sprague, Saproo, & Serences, 2015). These methods have shown that information about WM content features can be extracted from the sensory regions that respond to perception of that type of content (**Figure 1a**). This WM content information can be detected even when sustained average activation of the regions is absent or fails to distinguish between features (Harrison & Tong, 2009; Kiyonaga, Dowd, & Egner, 2017; Lorenc, Lee, Chen, & D'Esposito, 2015; Riggall & Postle, 2012; Serences, Ester, Vogel, & Awh, 2009; Sreenivasan, Curtis et al., 2014; Sreenivasan, Vytlacil, & D'Esposito, 2014). The consistent detection of WM feature information across sensory cortices has provided compelling support for the idea that WM representations are stored in the same cortical regions that process sensory input (Postle, 2015). Moreover, these multivariate classification and reconstruction techniques can detect the features of what is being remembered using classifiers that are trained on the activity patterns measured during stimulus perception. This provides further evidence that perceptual content and WM content are represented by shared activation substrates.

Population-level multivariate measures can also serve as an index of stimulus representation quality (Ester, Anderson, Serences, & Awh, 2013) and therefore reveal a more precise description of how WM and perceptual content compete. One example of this approach used an inverted encoding model analysis method to reconstruct the angle of remembered visual orientation stimuli under

a WM content reconstruction approach

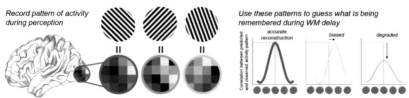

b Visual and parietal WM representation

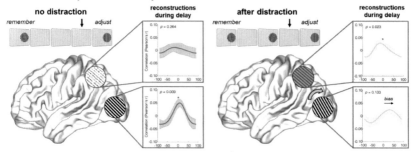

Figure 1 Perceptual input competes with WM content. (a) Left panel illustrates how different patterns of locally distributed activity, in this case across visual cortex voxels, correspond to different stimulus features, in this case the angle of oriented gratings. Right panel shows example orientation tuning functions or "reconstructions" of population-level stimulus representations during WM maintenance. (b) Results reproduced from Lorenc et al. (2018) illustrating WM stimulus reconstructions across visual and parietal regions during WM maintenance with and without distraction. After distraction (right), visual cortex representations were biased toward the angle of the distractor stimulus, while unbiased representations were detected in parietal cortex that were absent when there was no distraction (left).

different WM delay conditions (see **Figure 1**; see Sprague et al., 2018 for an overview of this method). When distractor orientation stimuli were presented during the delay, WM orientation reconstructions from visual cortical activity patterns were biased toward the angle of the distractor (Lorenc, Sreenivasan, Nee, Vandenbroucke, & D'Esposito, 2018). For instance, if an irrelevant distractor stimulus were oriented 45° clockwise relative to the WM stimulus, the visual cortical activity pattern associated with the WM representation looked like an activity pattern for a stimulus that was rotated ~15° clockwise relative to the WM sample. Thus, the feature information in the memory-related activity pattern was pulled in the direction of the distractor (see **Figure 1b**). This finding suggests that the memory representation itself can be corrupted (or modified) by perceptual distraction. This shift in neural WM stimulus reconstructions was also accompanied by an error in continuous report WM behavior: on average, participants recalled an angle biased slightly toward the angle of the distractor stimulus, suggesting that distraction may influence WM behavior by contaminating sensory WM representations.

However, we know from everyday experience that we can often simultaneously perceive and remember things successfully. How is this feasible if WM maintenance and perceptual input activate shared representations? One possibility may be the context-specific recruitment of additional regions to support WM when necessary. As an example from the orientation WM task described earlier, when a distractor was presented during WM maintenance, an unbiased (though less precise) WM content representation could be reconstructed from a region around the intraparietal sulcus (IPS; see **Figure 1b**). Yet such WM feature information was not discernible from IPS when distraction was absent (Lorenc et al., 2018; see also Bettencourt & Xu, 2016; Christophel, Iamshchinina, Yan, Allefeld, & Haynes, 2018; Rademaker, Chunharas, & Serences, 2019). Thus, WM may successfully rely on maintenance via high-fidelity representations in sensory cortex when no perceptual competition exists but may recruit additional regions and maintenance formats to protect WM content during perceptual competition (cf. Gayet, Paffen, & Stigchel, 2018). Indeed, WM-relevant representations at different levels of abstraction (e.g., precise stimulus identity, broad category, task-rule) are widely distributed across the cortex (Christophel, Klink, Spitzer, Roelfsema, & Haynes, 2017). WM representations in higher-order cortical regions may be coarser but able to bridge disruptions and reinstate high-fidelity sensory representations via top-down signals when necessary (Scimeca, Kiyonaga, & D'Esposito, 2018). Therefore, the representation of WM content in sensory cortex in no way precludes the representation of WM-relevant information in other regions. Instead, WM representations at several levels of the processing stream may integrate to promote successful WM maintenance.

Together, these findings demonstrate that perceptual input influences WM neural representations and behavior. The pattern of distractor influence on WM maintenance suggests that WM content is represented in the same cortical regions as perceptual input of the same type. WM is influenced more by perceptual input from the same sensory domain, input from the same category within the same sensory domain, and input with the same features within the same category – all suggesting that representations of both WM and perceptual content rely on the same cortical content maps, which interfere more when they overlap more. However, WM content information is represented in additional cortical regions when distracting perceptual input competes for representation

(Lorenc et al., 2018), and neural responses during WM maintenance are sensitive to the current task goals (Sreenivasan, Gratton et al., 2014; Yoon et al., 2006). These findings suggest that attentional control processes can adaptively manage simultaneous WM and perceptual processing demands in line with goals, and those control processes will be further examined in section 2.1.3 and in the second half of the Element.

2.1.2 WM Maintenance Influences Perceptual Attention

The previous section described how perceptual input can impact WM behavior and neural representations. If this does in fact occur because WM maintenance activates the same sensory representations as perceptual attention, then we should also observe the converse effect whereby WM content impacts perceptual processing. In support of that hypothesis, a great deal of evidence demonstrates that WM maintenance can increase perceptual sensitivity and attentional capture for features in the environment that match the WM content. Consider that you are sitting in your car at a stoplight, rehearsing your to-do list, envisioning the green shirt you need to pick up at the dry cleaner (imagine "green shirt, green shirt, green shirt"). If a person walks through the crosswalk wearing a green shirt, you will likely notice that person immediately, while others in blue suits or yellow dresses will not capture your attention. This can occur without consciously looking for a green shirt, and possibly at the expense of the more pressing task of monitoring the traffic. This sort of occurrence may also be beneficial, however, if the active memory content overlaps with currently relevant goals – for instance, if your immediate task were to pick up a green shirt–clad friend at the airport. In the laboratory, when a simple visual WM stimulus is maintained and a visual search is performed during the WM delay, search performance is best if the search target matches the features of the WM content and worst if the WM content matches search distractors (Dowd, Kiyonaga, Beck, & Egner, 2015; Dowd, Kiyonaga, Egner, & Mitroff, 2015; Kiyonaga, Egner, & Soto, 2012; Soto et al., 2008). For instance, if the task is to remember a yellow square for a WM test, a concurrent visual search during WM maintenance will be fastest when the target is located within a yellow square and slowest when a distractor is located within a yellow square (compared with a neutral condition wherein no yellow square appears; **Figure 2**). This type of modulation by WM occurs in the early stages of processing (Gayet et al., 2017; Hollingworth, Matsukura, & Luck, 2013; Saad & Silvanto, 2013; Soto, Wriglesworth, Bahrami-Balani, & Humphreys, 2010), which provides compelling evidence that the WM content is being represented in the same regions that process the sensory input.

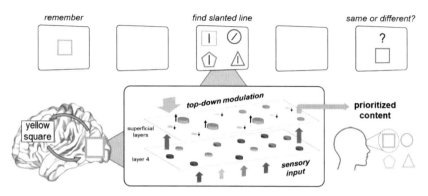

Figure 2 WM maintenance influences perceptual attention. The top panel shows a trial sequence from an example task used to examine attentional biases toward WM-matching stimuli. Participants remember a colored shape for a recognition test at the end of the trial. During the delay, they search for a target item (in this case a slanted line) that appears at the same location as a colored shape that may or may not match the WM content. This results in faster target detection when a WM match coincides with the slanted target, but slower target detection when a WM match coincides with a vertical distractor. The bottom panel illustrates a hypothesized mechanism by which perceptual attention may be captured by stimuli that match WM content. WM maintenance-related feedback increases neuronal firing associated with the WM content in the superficial and deep layers of visual cortex (van Kerkoerle et al., 2017), which then amplifies feed-forward sensory input from layer 4 that activates the same units.

Much like the impact of perceptual distraction on WM performance, the impact of visual WM maintenance on visual attentional task performance also scales with the similarity between the WM and perceptual content. For example, if the feature similarity (i.e., color distance) between WM content and visual search targets is continuously varied, the benefit of a WM-matching target or cost of a WM-matching distractor also continuously varies with similarity to the WM content (but see the next section for exceptions to this general tendency; Kiyonaga & Egner, 2016; Teng & Kravitz, 2019). That is, the more the mnemonic and perceptual representations overlap, the more drastic the influence on performance.

This interaction between WM and perceptual attention may arise because WM maintenance shifts visual receptive fields toward active WM content (Merrikhi et al., 2017) or amplifies WM content-responsive units, which preferentially amplifies the response to sensory input activating the same units (see

Figure 2). Indeed, the neural response associated with perceptual input is enhanced when it matches WM content (Gayet et al., 2017; Sreenivasan, Gratton et al., 2014). The modulation of sensory representations by WM maintenance may therefore increase sensitivity to matching features in the environment (Kiyonaga & Egner, 2013; Soto et al., 2010). As a consequence, while it may be trivial to filter out an irrelevant distraction that is unrelated to the WM content (Knight, Richard Staines, Swick, & Chao, 1999; Moran & Desimone, 1985), the activation of sensory cortices by WM maintenance might elevate responses to irrelevant input that matches the WM content and thereby promote attentional processing of that input (David, Hayden, Mazer, & Gallant, 2008). This is likely a product of the typically adaptive use of WM representations to guide perception and action, in that information matching active WM content should be prioritized because it would typically be relevant to the current situation. However, representations of goals or stimuli must often be maintained for future use while addressing more immediate demands. In this case, WM content may influence processing of those current demands. These involuntary interactions between WM and perception illuminate the structure of the WM system – WM content can bias perception and attention, even when it is maladaptive, which should only occur if WM maintenance and perceptual attention share content representations.

Finally, WM maintenance can reproduce established attentional phenomena as if the WM content were being perceived and attended in the external environment (Johnson et al., 2013; Kiyonaga & Egner, 2014b; Saad & Silvanto, 2013). For example, remembering a color word for a WM test can produce a Stroop-like effect as if the word were being currently perceived. It is well established that color-naming performance on the color-word Stroop task is slower when the meaning of the word is incompatible with the ink color (e.g., RED written in blue ink) as opposed to when it is compatible (e.g., BLUE written in blue; MacLeod, 1991). This slowing on incongruent trials is thought to be a result of a time-consuming attentional filtering process when there is competition between the stimulus and/or response representations for the color and word information (Cohen, Dunbar, & McClelland, 1990). This attentional filter can also be taxed by WM maintenance. That is, maintaining an incompatible color word in WM – rather than perceiving and reading it – can also produce comparable conflict in a simple perceptual judgment (Chen et al., 2017; Kiyonaga & Egner, 2014b; Pan, Han, & Zuo, 2019). When a color-word is remembered for a match/non-match recognition task (e.g., remember "RED"), naming the color of a visual stimulus during the WM delay (e.g., a blue rectangular patch) is dramatically slowed if the WM sample word and perceptual input are incompatible. Therefore, WM content can impact perceptual attention much like perceived stimuli, providing further evidence that it not only activates the same representations but also operates by the same attentional processes. The next section will further explore these attentional processes.

2.1.3 The Attentional State of WM Content Modulates Its Influence on Perception

The biased competition model describes how two (or more) perceived stimuli compete for neural representation. The previous sections of this Element demonstrated that perceptual stimuli can also compete with WM content, as would be expected if they shared cortical representations. A critical prediction of the biased competition model, however, is that top-down attentional signals can reduce this competition by biasing the neural response in favor of the selected stimulus (i.e., the one that wins the competition; Desimone & Duncan, 1995). In other words, the neural activity associated with the attended stimulus is amplified or increased in "gain" (Hillyard, Vogel, & Luck, 1998; Reynolds & Chelazzi, 2004), and it is therefore less susceptible to competition from unattended stimuli. Likewise, WM content does not always interfere with perceptual input (Woodman & Luck, 2007), and we are typically able to handle simultaneous WM maintenance and perceptual attention demands in daily life. One context in which WM maintenance and perceptual attention may not impede each other is when the content features are different enough that they are segregated in cortex. However, even when WM maintenance and perceptual attention operate over similar content, competition effects between them can be modest (e.g., Bettencourt & Xu, 2016). In this case, top-down signals may bias the competition between mnemonic and perceptual demands in line with goals, therefore limiting the interference that might occur without such feedback. That is, evidence for interference may sometimes be absent in behavior, not because WM and perception rely on separate representations and resources, but because attentional control mechanisms are engaged to limit the competition between them. If this is the case, representations of WM content should be modulated by attention just like perceptual stimuli, and attentionally prioritized representations should drive behavior. The following sections will examine two related hypotheses about the relationship between WM mainten-ance and perceptual attention: (1) that the activation state (or gain) of WM representations can be selectively modulated based on goals, much like representations of perceptual stimuli, and (2) that the activation state of WM representations will determine whether they compete with perceptual stimuli and guide behavior.

Biased Competition Suppresses Nearby Representations

When perceptual attention is directed at a particular stimulus, processing for that location or feature is enhanced while processing for nearby stimuli is diminished (Cutzu & Tsotsos, 2003; Hopf et al., 2006). In visual attention, this center-surround suppression is thought to be implemented in V1 via feedback signals from higher regions (Nassi, Lomber, & Born, 2013). Namely, it is considered to be a product of top-down modulation rather than an inherent property of local neuronal interactions. This attentional center-surround modulation is thought to confer a sharpened demarcation between task-relevant and task-irrelevant stimuli (Tsotsos et al., 1995), in line with the assumption that attention biases the competitive relationship between stimuli to adaptively favor task-relevant stimulus features. However, this results in less efficient selection of two similar features (as opposed to dissimilar ones; Störmer & Alvarez, 2014) because stimuli that are represented nearby in cortex have overlapping inhibitory surrounds (Franconeri et al., 2013). This suggests a more specific mechanism for the competition between similar stimuli that was described in the first section of this Element: similar WM content and perceptual input can interfere with each other because they mutually suppress each other through surround-inhibition. As described earlier, competition can occur between multiple perceptual stimuli or between WM and perceptual content. It follows that the surround suppression principle should also operate among simultaneously maintained WM representations. Indeed, two color WM stimuli mutually inhibit each other and result in worse recognition performance when they have more similar hues (compared to two stimuli that are farther apart in color space; Kiyonaga & Egner, 2016), and WM for multiple items is better when they are more spatially distant (Emrich & Ferber, 2012; Umemoto, Drew, Ester, & Awh, 2010; also see Oberauer & Lin, 2017; Pertzov, Manohar, & Husain, 2017). This suggests that WM representations are characterized by an inhibitory surround that suppresses the signal associated with nearby – and therefore potentially confusable – representations, just as in perceptual attention. As such, a WM representation that is selectively attended should be amplified, while representations of highly similar stimuli should be diminished, and the attended representation should beat out the competition for processing.

Accordingly, this competitive modulation also dictates the influence of WM maintenance on perceptual attention. As described earlier, when a visual task is performed during WM maintenance, visual stimuli that match the WM content can capture attention. However, visual stimuli that are very similar (but not identical) to an attended WM item – and should therefore fall within the inhibitory penumbra of the WM representation – are instead deprioritized and fail to capture attention (Kiyonaga & Egner, 2016). Yet less similar (presumably noncompeting) stimuli do produce the attentional bias, albeit to a lesser extent than identical stimuli. That is, stimuli that are identical to the WM content capture visual attention, while very similar stimuli (~10°–30° away in color space) do not. Related stimuli that are beyond the bounds of the presumed inhibitory surround then show a graded influence on visual attention that decreases as the representations get less and less similar. Much like how WM performance is better for representations that are distinct from perceptual input, visual processing is better for stimuli that are distinct from the current WM content. This suggests that attending to the WM content biases processing in favor of the WM representation, at the expense of potentially interfering representations, thereby reducing competition with the WM content. This is corroborated by the observation that fMRI responses to potentially interfering visual stimuli during WM maintenance are suppressed in visual cortex in a similar fashion (Sneve, Sreenivasan, Alnæs, Endestad, & Magnussen, 2015). Moreover, a stronger behavioral suppression of stimuli that resemble the WM sample also relates to better WM performance (Kiyonaga & Egner, 2016). This suggests that the inhibitory surround mechanism does in fact serve to enhance the relevant representation in WM maintenance, just as it does in perceptual attention. In sum, WM representations compete with one another like multiple perceptual stimuli would. They are characterized by the same center-surround mechanism to reduce competition, and this attentional modulation results in diminished processing of perceptual input that may be confusable with WM representations. These observations highlight the adaptive role of biased competition within and between WM and perception: to inhibit potentially confusable content and prioritize the representations that are most relevant to current goals. The following sections will describe other conditions under which WM representations may be modulated by selective attention, and how that modulation influences the behavioral impact of WM maintenance.

Top-Down Attention Modulates the Gain of WM Representations

The center-surround modulation previously described can amplify relevant low-level stimulus responses in early visual regions. Perceptual attention has also been shown to amplify the neural response associated with complex stimulus categories and diminish that associated with a simultaneously presented but unattended stimulus (O'Craven, Downing, & Kanwisher, 1999). Analogously, when multiple WM items are maintained, attention can be selectively focused among those items, and this prioritization is reflected in the neural activity associated with each item. Specifically, when WM content is "actively

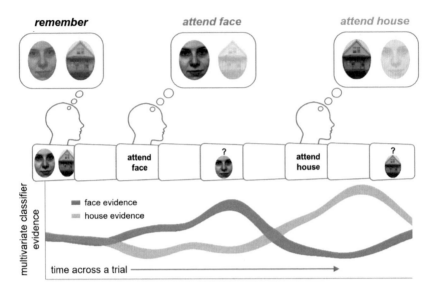

Figure 3 Top-down attention modulates the gain of WM representations.
An example task and timeline of WM stimulus representation information when attention alternates among multiple remembered stimuli. Colored traces represent evidence that a given stimulus category is being maintained, based on the multivariate pattern of brain activity. Face representation evidence (orange trace) is relatively increased when face information is cued as most task-relevant. When house information is cued instead, then house representation evidence (blue trace) is increased relative to face evidence.

maintained" in the focus of (internally oriented) attention, evidence for the associated representations can be detected in distributed multivariate patterns of brain activity (see **Figure 1a**). However, those patterns typically become uninformative when attention is directed away (**Figure 3**; LaRocque, Lewis-Peacock, & Postle, 2014; Lewis-Peacock, Drysdale, & Postle, 2014). This can be examined, for instance, by giving two oriented gratings as WM samples and then using a retrospective cue to indicate that only one of the samples is the relevant item to be remembered. In this case, multivariate classifier evidence for that prioritized item persists in visual, parietal, and frontal regions, while evidence for the other (now-irrelevant) item is suppressed below baseline (Lorenc et al., 2020). Therefore, the gain of WM representations is sensitive to the task-relevance of the content and is modulated by selective attention in much the same way as representations of perceptual stimuli (cf. Griffin & Nobre, 2003; Lepsien & Nobre, 2006, 2007; Nelissen, Stokes, Nobre, & Rushworth, 2013).

This and other similar observations have led to the proposal that there may be multiple "activation states" of WM representation (Rose et al., 2016; Sprague, Ester, & Serences, 2016; Stokes, 2015; Wolff, Jochim, Akyürek, & Stokes, 2017; Yu, Teng, & Postle, 2020). In this framework, attended WM content is readily available for cognitive action – a neural and behavioral state that can be distinguished from other lower priority WM activation states (Nee & Jonides, 2008). If the observed interactions between WM and perceptual content (described in the first two sections (2.1.1 and 2.1.2) of this Element) serve a typically adaptive purpose, WM content that is activated in the focus of attention should preferentially drive behavior (Myers et al., 2017; Olivers, Peters, Houtkamp, & Roelfsema, 2011). Consistent with that hypothesis, only cued (i.e., prioritized) WM items bias perceptual attention toward items with matching features, whereas "unattended" WM items fail to capture attention (Mallett & Lewis-Peacock, 2018; van Moorselaar, Theeuwes, & Olivers, 2014). This highlights that the activity patterns associated with WM representations are modulated by attention (just like perceptual stimuli), and that the activation state (or gain) of WM content may determine its influence on externally geared processes. In other words, attention modulates the gain of representations, and that modulation biases the competition in favor of the amplified representation.

WM Maintenance Processes Compete with Perceptual Attentional Processes

The previous sections have focused on the stimulus-specific interplay between WM and perceptual *content* – that is, how representations of WM and perceptual stimuli impact each other, presumably because they overlap in sensory cortices. However, if WM maintenance and perceptual attention employ the same top-down modulation processes (over the same sensory representations), then WM maintenance should also compete with perceptual attention for shared top-down resources. This systems-level processing competition should in turn influence the integrity of the local content representations, because those representations are activated by top-down modulation. Indeed, goal-directed attention among either perceptual stimuli or WM representations engages a highly similar fronto-parietal network (Gazzaley & Nobre, 2012), suggesting that they might rely on shared processes. Moreover, perceptual processing demands can impair WM behavior. For example, a time-consuming concurrent task during WM maintenance (i.e., a "dual-task" context) can impair WM performance, even when there is little feature overlap between WM and perceptual stimuli (Barrouillet, Portrat, & Camos, 2011; Kiyonaga & Egner, 2014a, 2014b; Watanabe & Funahashi, 2015). This suggests that WM suffers when attention is directed away from maintenance. Similarly, an intervening perceptual task in a different content domain taxes WM performance more during high WM load (e.g., face and scene image processing can impair digit span for greater numbers of digits; Rissman, Gazzaley, & D'Esposito, 2009). These findings suggest that WM maintenance is achieved via domain-general top-down modulation, and that this processing resource faces competition when attention is taxed in multiple domains. However, EEG signals can discriminate between spatial attention and working memory storage (Feldman-Wustefeld, Vogel, & Awh, 2018; Hakim et al., 2019). Thus, these are not interchangeable processes but likely coordinate with each other to prioritize relevant information.

If WM maintenance competes with perceptual attention for top-down signaling, then neural representations of WM content should be modulated by concurrent perceptual attentional demand. Indeed, just as attention toward individual items in WM can influence the neural response pattern and behavioral impact of WM content (e.g., Lorenc et al., 2020; Mallett & Lewis-Peacock, 2018), WM content is similarly modulated by shifting attention between WM maintenance and a perceptual attention task; namely, the quality of distributed neural WM representation patterns (see **Figure 1a**) fluctuates as attention is directed at WM maintenance vs. perceptual attentional processing (e.g., Derrfuss, Ekman, Hanke, Tittgemeyer, & Fiebach, 2017). More specifically, while the category of visual WM content can be detected during a delay-spanning visual search task (across the extrastriate regions that respond to perception of the WM categories), the accuracy of decoding that WM information decreases when the visual task is more perceptually attentionally demanding (Kiyonaga, Dowd, et al., 2017). Even when the perceptual task involves distinct content categories from the WM aspect of the task, detectable WM-related information can be degraded if domain-general attention is taxed. That is, attentionally demanding perceptual tasks may detract attention from WM maintenance, dampening the gain of WM representations. Task-irrelevant interruption similarly disrupts EEG markers of WM activation (Hakim et al., 2020). Furthermore, occupying attention during WM maintenance also eliminates the attentional capture by WM-matching visual stimuli (Kiyonaga & Egner, 2014a). Specifically, when an attentionally demanding perceptual processing task is completed during WM maintenance – which has been shown to diminish the discriminability of sensory WM representation patterns – the involuntary influence of WM content on perceptual attention is also diminished. This is consistent with the idea that the gain of WM representations influences their degree of competition with perceptual representations and provides further evidence that attentional state determines which representations win the competition for processing.

Finally, WM representations can be strategically modulated depending on their predictive relevance to concurrent perceptual processing. The evidence reviewed earlier shows that a WM representation's gain is modulated when attention is either explicitly cued among WM representations (e.g., Lorenc et al., 2020) or when WM maintenance competes with perceptual attention demands (e.g., Kiyonaga, Dowd et al., 2017). However, statistical properties of the task context can also promote attentional prioritization (or de-prioritization) of internally maintained WM content. This parallels reliable effects in spatial perceptual attention, which can be strategically oriented toward locations that are most likely to contain task-relevant information (Posner, 1980; Posner & Snyder, 1975). Likewise, when WM representations are more likely to be relevant and useful in a visual attention task (see **Figure 2**), they can be enhanced. For instance, in a task context when WM content is likely to coincide with a visual search target – and is therefore predictably helpful – the magnitude of the attentional capture benefit can be increased. Conversely, when WM content is likely to coincide with a visual search distractor – and is therefore predictably disruptive – the magnitude of the attentional capture cost can be decreased (Carlisle & Woodman, 2011; Kiyonaga et al., 2012; Kiyonaga, Korb, Lucas, Soto, & Egner, 2014; Soto, Greene, Kiyonaga, Rosenthal, & Egner, 2012). This sort of strategic modulation can also reduce competition between WM and perceptual content in a WM Stroop task (described earlier), or between WM content and action goals. When a verbal WM sample is more likely to conflict with a perceptual color judgment task or a cued movement task, the competition effect is reduced (Kiyonaga & Egner, 2014b; Miller et al., in press). However, when WM content is less relevant to perceptual goals, WM perform-ance is also slower and marked by higher guessing rates, suggesting that the WM representation is suppressed to prevent it from maladaptively biasing visual attention (Dowd, Kiyonaga, Beck et al., 2015; Kiyonaga & Egner, 2014b; Kiyonaga et al., 2012). These findings suggest that the gain of WM content can be enhanced or suppressed according to its usefulness to ongoing behavior.

2.2 Previously Perceived or Remembered Information Influences WM and Perception

The preceding sections described the influence between concurrent WM and perceptual demands. However, perceived or remembered information from the recent past can also proactively bias current perception and memory (Kiyonaga, Scimeca, Bliss, & Whitney, 2017). In a spatial delayed response task, for instance, remembered locations are biased toward the angle of recently remembered stimuli from the previous trial (Bliss, Sun, & D'Esposito, 2017). This temporal smoothing, or "serial dependence," is thought to facilitate a cohesive perceptual or mnemonic experience that is robust to disruptions. That is, since visual WM maintains representations that bridge changes in the retinal image (e.g., from eye movements, blinks, occlusions), this may result in biasing of incoming perceptual (and mnemonic) information toward recent representations. Although this bias can be helpful when it is adaptive to integrate across successive stimuli (i.e., to improve signal-to-noise), it can be maladaptive when previous information is no longer relevant to current goals. For instance, verbal WM is slower and more error prone if a non-match probe item belonged to a recent memory set (D'Esposito, Postle, Jonides, & Smith, 1999; Jonides & Nee, 2006). However, like "retroactive interference" from competing perceptual input on current WM content, this proactive interference from recent stimuli can be modulated by contextual factors and attentional control.

As with the influence of perceptual input on WM maintenance (and vice versa), serial dependence is sensitive to the similarity between past and current stimuli – once that difference exceeds a certain magnitude, the bias disappears (Bliss et al., 2017; Fischer & Whitney, 2014; Kiyonaga et al., 2017). Similar content may produce a stronger bias because it is more likely to be relevant to current goals, while the influence from (presumably) less-relevant dissimilar content is dampened. The neural mechanisms underlying serial dependence in behavior (or its modulation) are poorly understood, although computational modeling suggests that sustained WM activity drives changes in synaptic weighting that influence later stimulus activity (Bliss & D'Esposito, 2017). Recent electrophysiological data augments this idea, showing that interactions between prefrontal persistent activity and "activity-silent" traces engender the bias (Barbosa et al., 2020). Neural signatures of proactive interference also emerge in the same sensory cortical regions that perceptually process the remembered content (John-Saaltink, Kok, Lau, & Lange, 2016; Oztekin & Badre, 2011; Papadimitriou, White, & Snyder, 2016), which further suggests that the interactions between WM and perceptual content arise from their shared reliance on the same cortical substrates.

Just as active WM content can bias perception and attention toward similar perceptual stimuli, the lingering activation of previously relevant stimuli may result in heightened sensitivity for related information in the environment. This would prioritize perception and WM encoding for incoming information that is most relevant to the current situation. However, interference between enduring previous representations and current goals may trigger the engagement of attentional control processes to minimize its impact. For instance, ventrolateral

PFC, a possible source of feedback signals, is activated by interference from recently remembered (but now irrelevant) verbal content (D'Esposito et al., 1999), and damage to this region is associated with a greater degree of proactive interference (Thompson-Schill et al., 2002). This suggests that top-down modulation may segregate competing representations to dampen maladaptive serial dependence. Therefore, the influence from past representations also reveals competition between perceptual attention and WM, as well as the attentional control processes that reduce that competition.

2.3 Interim Summary

The principles that govern perceptual attention also govern WM maintenance, as well as the interactions between WM and perceptual content. WM maintenance is reflected in brain activity across regions that respond to perceptual processing of the maintained stimulus features, suggesting that WM content is stored in sensory representations. Attentional modulation of WM (and perceptual) content may be achieved via top-down feedback from higher-order regions to sensory-processing regions. However, these feedback signals are disrupted by distraction or intervening attentional demands. In such cases, WM storage may require the recruitment of additional regions to protect WM representations from interference. In this way, representations at different levels – stored by distributed brain regions – may support flexible maintenance in the face of competition. How do these distributed regions communicate and coordinate attentional control when WM maintenance faces competition? The rest of the Element will address this question.

3 Network Interactions Support Attentional Control of WM

We have reviewed considerable evidence that WM maintenance recruits sensory representations. However, WM maintenance activity – or "delay activity" – is also observed across many brain regions beyond sensory cortex (Sreenivasan & D'Esposito, 2019). Namely, fronto-parietal activation is essentially ubiquitous in studies of WM (Constantinidis & Klingberg, 2016; Curtis & D'Esposito, 2003; D'Esposito & Postle, 2015; Eriksson, Vogel, Lansner, Bergström, & Nyberg, 2015). If sensory cortex is responsible for storing high-fidelity representations of WM content, how does the distributed activity observed across the brain during WM maintenance – for example, in fronto-parietal regions – relate to and integrate with sensory representations?

Across many studies, it has become clear that WM maintenance emerges from interactions between the fronto-parietal cortex and numerous other regions (Curtis & D'Esposito, 2003; D'Esposito, 2007; D'Esposito &

Grossman, 1996; Sreenivasan, Curtis et al., 2014). Moreover, interactions at the level of large-scale brain networks have increasingly been found to play an essential role in cognition (Behrmann & Plaut, 2013; Pessoa, 2012; Power & Petersen, 2013). The first half of this Element introduced the idea that goal-oriented attentional control processes can modulate WM representations to limit the detrimental impacts of competition. We will now examine how such top-down modulation is achieved by systems-level interactions across distributed brain regions and networks. The following sections will build toward the idea that attentional control and WM main-tenance occur within a flexible network architecture that balances internal goals with contextual demands.

3.1 Fronto-Parietal Regions Play an Attentional Role in WM Maintenance

Here we review evidence that fronto-parietal regions play a modulatory role to sustain sensory cortical representations. In one of the earliest demonstrations of the importance of lateral PFC to WM, monkeys with bilateral frontal lesions (around the principal sulcus) were shown to be impaired in delayed response tasks (Jacobsen, 1935). This impairment suggested that the lesioned regions of frontal cortex were necessary for short-term memory. In a remarkable repro-duction and extension of that initial finding, however, monkeys with frontal lesions were only severely impaired in a delayed response task when the lights were on, while no impairment was observed in total darkness (Malmo, 1942). The animals appeared unable to inhibit visible distracting input, suggesting that the prefrontal damage produced a specific inability to suppress irrelevant sensory information, consequently impairing performance. That is, the deficit produced by frontal lesions was attentional rather than mnemonic. Human lesion studies have corroborated the theory that lateral PFC is inessential to pure WM maintenance but is necessary in the face of additional attentional demands (such as distraction; D'Esposito, Cooney, Gazzaley, Gibbs, & Postle, 2006; D'Esposito & Postle, 1999). Human fMRI studies also demonstrate that lateral PFC is implicated in WM maintenance during heightened attentional demands – such as manipulation of WM content – as opposed to simple WM maintenance (D'Esposito et al., 1998; D'Esposito, Postle, Ballard, & Lease, 1999; Postle, Berger, & D'Esposito, 1999). Parietal cortex has similarly been implicated in a range of attentional processes during WM, like attentional orienting toward WM representations and suppression of irrelevant distraction (Magen, Emmanouil, McMains, Kastner, & Treisman, 2009; McNab & Klingberg, 2008; Sauseng et al., 2009). Thus, human and animal studies have converged on the idea that frontal and parietal regions are engaged during WM maintenance to filter distracting input and manage otherwise competing attentional demands (Friedman-Hill, Robertson, Desimone, & Ungerleider, 2003; Jacob & Nieder, 2014; Knight et al., 1999; Moran & Desimone, 1985; Postle, 2005; Suzuki & Gottlieb, 2013; Watanabe & Funahashi, 2015).

It is clear that the fronto-parietal regions that are implicated in WM are also engaged by many non-WM functions. For example, lateral PFC regions that are activated during maintenance and manipulation of WM content are also activated by tasks with no WM demand (D'Esposito, Ballard, Aguirre, & Zarahn, 1998). Similar regions of lateral PFC are also activated during retrieval from long-term memory, especially when retrieval requires greater detail (Ranganath, Johnson, & D'Esposito, 2000), suggesting that the activation may be a response to the higher attentional demands of precise retrieval. Likewise, lateral PFC responds to the retrieval of semantic knowledge, especially when selecting information among competing alternatives (Thompson-Schill, D'Esposito, Aguirre, & Farah, 1997; Thompson-Schill, D'Esposito, & Kan, 1999). This suggests that lateral PFC can bias or gate relevant memory representations from posterior cortex in the face of competition. Combined with many other findings, these observations reinforce the idea that frontal cortex (along with parietal cortex) conveys top-down signals to bias, manipulate, protect, or otherwise control distributed cortical WM content representations (Curtis & D'Esposito, 2003; Miller & D'Esposito, 2005; Sreenivasan, Curtis et al., 2014). That is, fronto-parietal regions are the source of top-down signals that can modulate sensory representations.

While a full review of all the functions of fronto-parietal regions during WM is beyond the scope of this Element, it is important to note that many studies find evidence for stimulus-specific WM content representations in these regions (Bettencourt & Xu, 2016; Christophel, Hebart, & Haynes, 2012; Christophel et al., 2018; Ester, Sprague, & Serences, 2015; Leavitt et al., 2017; Riley & Constantinidis, 2016; Sprague et al., 2016). These findings suggest that fronto-parietal regions are involved in WM storage, rather than just attentional control functions. Indeed, it is likely that WM representations at many different levels of abstraction are stored across the cortex (Christophel et al., 2017), and heteromodal fronto-parietal regions can represent many types of information (D'Esposito, 2007; Duncan, 2010; Miller & Cohen, 2001; Rigotti et al., 2013). Therefore, the necessity of fronto-parietal regions to attentional control does not preclude their involvement in WM content storage. As described in the first half of the Element, while WM maintenance recruits sensory representations, these may be vulnerable to disruption (Kiyonaga, Dowd et al., 2017; Lorenc et al., 2018). Thus,

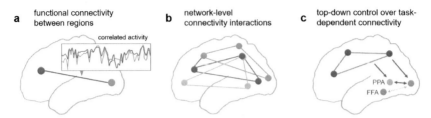

Figure 4 A schematic of large-scale distributed activity for WM maintenance and control. (a) Two functionally connected regions display correlated time-series of activity. Frontal regions are often functionally connected with stimulus representation regions during WM maintenance, which may reflect top-down modulation. (b) A set of functionally connected regions can form a network, and networks may communicate with each other for attentional control and WM maintenance. Networks may interact with each other through overlapping nodes (e.g., sub-networks for several functions may share the same parietal node), or distinct nodes from separable networks may interact with each other to coordinate activity among the networks (e.g., frontal nodes of two separate networks may be connected with each other). (c) Schematic illustration of the results of Hwang et al. (2018), whereby fronto-parietal regions modulate information flow within sensory representation sub-networks. In this example, place images are task-relevant, and connectivity between PPA and early visual regions is associated with fronto-parietal network activity.

a network of regions beyond sensory cortex may be flexibly recruited for storage depending on current demands. The next sections of the Element will further examine the brain-wide communication and organization functions that support this flexible WM maintenance.

3.2 WM Maintenance Arises from Interactions between a Network of Brain Regions

Functional connectivity is a measure of correlated fluctuations in fMRI BOLD signal between brain regions, and a means of gauging which areas may be communicating or coordinating activity (**Figure 4a**). During WM maintenance, fronto-parietal regions are functionally connected with stimulus representation regions, suggesting that fronto-parietal regions may be the source of top-down signals. For instance, language-sensitive regions increase activity as verbal WM load increases, and this modulation is accompanied by increased functional connectivity with the left middle frontal gyrus (MFG) (Fiebach, Rissman, & D'Esposito, 2006). This suggests that communication with frontal regions guides sustained activation of inferotemporal language representations. Indeed, granger causality analyses suggest that the direction of communication is from more frontal to more posterior regions (Sneve, Magnussen, Alnæs, Endestad, & D'Esposito, 2013). Brain stimulation has also causally confirmed the top-down modulatory role of prefrontal regions during WM maintenance. For instance, when inhibitory transcranial magnetic stimulation (TMS) is applied to the left inferior frontal gyrus (IFG), the selectivity of category-specific responses is reduced in extrastriate regions-of-interest(ROIs) during WM for face or scene images (Lee & D'Esposito, 2012). That is, while patterns of activity across voxels in face- and place-responsive ROIs typically discriminate between the remembered categories, that discriminability is reduced after TMS perturbs IFG activity. This provides strong causal evidence that lateral PFC modulates WM-related activity in sensory regions.

3.2.1 WM Network Interactions Are Distributed and Flexible

Functional interactions during WM are observed across multiple connected areas – they are not limited to correlated activity between a single prefrontal "control" node and a posterior "storage" node. During WM maintenance of face stimuli, for instance, the fusiform face area is functionally connected with superior frontal sulcus, parietal, pre-motor, pre-SMA(supplementary motor area), and caudate regions, in addition to the MFG (Gazzaley, Rissman, & D'Esposito, 2004). In other words, a distributed *network* of regions underlies WM maintenance. Moreover, the pattern of connectivity across WM-relevant networks is modulated by task goals and attentional competition. For instance, during an n-back WM task for either faces or scenes – while both categories are presented in a continuous stream – lateral PFC is more coupled with face-processing regions when faces are relevant to the WM task, and more coupled with scene-processing regions when scenes are relevant to the task (i.e., when the category is attended vs. ignored; Gazzaley et al., 2007; see also Feredoes et al., 2011; Hwang et al., 2018).

While face WM maintenance is associated with connectivity between lateral PFC and fusiform face area(FFA), that profile shifts to hippocampus-FFA connectivity when WM load increases (Rissman, Gazzaley, & D'Esposito, 2008). Therefore, task demands can modulate the affiliations between regions – or nodes – of the WM network, which may be how attentional control is implemented. A WM network is composed of distributed but interacting nodes that may play different roles (e.g., feedback signaling, storage, interference resolution), and those nodes can shift in their current relevance to performance. Depending on the task conditions (e.g., response modality, concurrent demands), networks for WM maintenance may also need to interact with networks for other functions to successfully guide action (**Figure 4b**). Rather than just quantitative changes in "engagement," for instance, WM networks may reconfigure by shifting connectivity relationships to overcome competition within any particular region or network.

The distributed regions that coactivate during WM underlie a multilevel architecture for maintenance. Within this architecture, several sub-networks and network nodes coordinate to modulate representations at several levels of the processing stream. For instance, while we described earlier that fronto-parietal signals modulate the gain or tuning in sensory representation regions, these signals may also modulate *information flow* within sensory perception and representation sub-networks of the brain (**Figure 4c**). More specifically, a distributed set of fronto-parietal regions displays increased activity during an n-back WM task, and that increased activity corresponds with increased functional connectivity between early visual and extrastriate regions (Hwang, Shine, & D'Esposito, 2018). That is, the coupling strength between early visual cortex and category-specific extrastriate regions (FFA or parahippocampal place area(PPA) during face or scene WM, respectively) increases when the region's preferred category is relevant and when WM demands increase. That task-modulated connectivity between visual subregions is associated with increased activity in fronto-parietal network regions. This suggests that the fronto-parietal regions convey top-down signals that modulate local communication between sensory processing and stimulus representation regions (Hwang et al., 2018). Top-down attentional control may therefore modulate WM maintenance by modulating local patterns of activity and connectivity in sensory cortical representations. In other words, connectivity within lower-order networks for stimulus processing and representation may be coordinated by higher-order networks for top-down modulation (**Figure 4c**).

3.2.2 Oscillations May Carry Information throughout Networks

Although correlated fMRI activity between regions is thought to reflect communication and coordination, it does not specify a mechanism of information transfer. Oscillations in the neuronal extracellular field may provide that fundamental mechanism (Buzsáki & Draguhn, 2004; Fries, 2015). Rhythmic activity at different frequencies, moreover, may serve long-range vs. local interactions for distinct cognitive functions. For instance, neurophysiological recordings in nonhuman primates have shown that directed coherence of beta frequency oscillations, from frontal to parietal cortex, mediates top-down attention during a feature-based visual search task (Buschman & Miller, 2007). On the other hand, directed coherence of gamma oscillations, from parietal to frontal cortex, mediates stimulus-driven attention in a pop-out detection task. This suggests that lower-frequency oscillations may convey top-down signals over the long-range to coordinate and bias local high-frequency activity for bottom-up stimulus processing. Online rhythmic TMS, delivered at task-relevant oscillatory frequencies during task performance, can be used to causally test these proposed oscillatory mechanisms (Albouy, Weiss, Baillet, & Zatorre, 2017; Sauseng et al., 2009). In a recent application of this approach, for instance, slower-frequency beta TMS, applied to frontal and parietal targets, influenced accuracy in a task with top-down control demands (i.e., visual selection among competing alternatives; Riddle, Hwang, Cellier, Dhanani, & D'Esposito, 2019). Conversely, high-frequency gamma TMS influenced bottom-up attentional response times. Together, these findings provide causal evidence in humans to corroborate the earlier monkey findings (i.e., Buschman & Miller, 2007).

Human intracranial electrocorticograhy (ECoG) also illuminates a multilevel architecture of oscillatory WM network interactions. For instance, attentional control demands (to maintain multiple task goals across time) influence both (a) the amplitude of high-frequency gamma activity *within* local frontal subregions as well as (b) the synchronization of lower-frequency theta *between* frontal subregions (Voytek et al., 2015). Theta-gamma phase-amplitude coupling between these regions also increases with attentional control demands, further demonstrating that low-frequency frontal rhythms may coordinate higher-frequency local neuronal activity. Therefore, coordinated oscillatory activity may represent the mechanism for information flow throughout brain networks (de Vries, Slagter, & Olivers, 2020), whereby top-down attentional control signals modulate local sensory representation dynamics.

In sum, long-range top-down signals (a) modulate the gain of connected regions, (b) modulate the selectivity or tuning of stimulus representation responses, and (c) modulate the information flow between other connected regions or sub-networks. This top-down modulation arises from networks of interacting nodes, whose connectivity relationships shift flexibly with changing task demands. In the first section of this Element, we suggested that increased attentional demands – such as those arising from distraction or a dual-task interference – may necessitate engagement of distinct regions to bolster the WM content. This flexible selective recruitment of different brain regions can be understood as reconfiguration of different networks (which we will explore in section 3.4). Therefore, networks adapting their connectivity structure may be how WM content is protected from new perceptual input or concurrent attentional demands. For instance, an irrelevant distraction in a different stimulus domain might promote strengthening of the relationship between WM maintenance and stimulus representation networks to increase the gain of the WM representation (Feredoes, Heinen, Weiskopf, Ruff, & Driver, 2011). Alternatively, a perceptually similar distraction might instead shift that connectivity with sensory regions in a manner that limits interference (Yoon et al., 2006). In that case, WM storage may rely on higher-order, categorical levels of representation (e.g., Lorenc et al., 2018), thereby transferring the storage role to different network nodes, and perhaps engaging distinct networks to support maintenance in the face of competition. WM maintenance and attentional control may therefore be better explained at the level of interactions among networks, rather than just at the level of individual regions, or the connectivity between two regions (**Figure 4**). The next section will further examine the adaptive multilevel architecture of WM networks.

3.3 Hierarchically Organized Networks May Promote Robust and Efficient Attentional Control

Any given task can be made up of several sub-tasks, where the overarching task goal must be maintained in WM while a number of sub-goals (which must also be held in WM) are implemented. For instance, the abstract task goal of "set the table" guides a series of sub-tasks, like retrieving silverware, plates, and glasses. Moreover, the implementation of specific sub-tasks may be context dependent, for instance, hinging on whether it is a casual weeknight dinner or a formal holiday gathering. In this case, the overarching goal of "set the table" would be at the top of the abstraction hierarchy, while the context-dependent rule of "if it's a weeknight, use acrylic; if it's a holiday, use china" would be intermediate, and the immediate stimulus-response mapping between retrieving and placing a (context-appropriate) plate would be the most concrete. FMRI (Badre & D'Esposito, 2007), lesion (Badre, Hoffman, Cooney, & D'Esposito, 2009), and ECoG studies (Voytek et al., 2015) have demonstrated that a hierarchical organization of representation abstraction exists across the frontal lobes and likely extends to posterior association regions as well (Choi, Drayna, & Badre, 2018). Specifically, more anterior regions of frontal cortex generally support more abstract levels of control (or representation), suggesting a rostral-to-caudal flow of processing to translate higher-order goals into context-appropriate actions. Anterior frontal regions are anatomically and physiologically well positioned to serve this function as they display more diffuse projections and less laminar differentiation (Badre & D'Esposito, 2009), consistent with more integrative processing and high-dimensional representation.

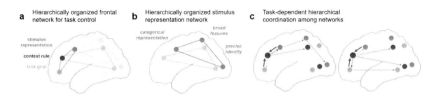

Figure 5 Hierarchically organized networks. (a) Frontal cortex displays a rostro-caudal gradient of representational abstraction whereby more anterior regions represent task control goals that are the most conceptually broad or temporally extended. Those regions must interact to coordinate the different levels of control and guide action. (b) A hierarchically organized frontal cortex network for task control interacts with several hierarchically organized sub-networks to carry out each level of control. For example, stimulus representation information is also represented by distributed regions at several levels of abstraction, and the context-appropriate engagement of these stimulus representation nodes would be coordinated by interaction with the frontal task control network. (c) Two examples of possible network communication schemes. Mid-lateral PFC may combine abstract and concrete information from anterior and posterior regions of the frontal network and communicate integrated signals to task-relevant networks. Depending on the current task demands, different sub-networks and nodes will be engaged.

Together, these frontal regions form a hierarchically organized network for task control (**Figure 5a**).

In addition to a hierarchical organization of representational abstraction within a frontal network, a *nested* organization of goal, task, and stimulus representations across other brain networks would promote efficient action selection. That is, while the task of retrieving and placing dishes on the table falls within the most concrete level of task control, those dishes may be further organized depending on their functions. For example, one might organize their cabinets by dishes for eating vs. drinking, and then further organize their drinkware into coffee mugs, drinking glasses, stemware, and so on, rather than putting all dishes for all needs on the same chaotic shelf. Likewise, while overarching task control goals may be represented at different levels of abstraction across frontal cortex (**Figure 5a**), stimulus properties may also be represented at multiple levels of abstraction within a stimulus representation network (e.g., green network in **Figure 5b**). For instance, different cortical regions represent information about the sensory domain (i.e., visual), object category (i.e., face), broad stimulus features (i.e., female), and a precise integrated representation (i.e., specific identity). This sort of nested hierarchical organization would also be displayed across other sub-networks for the component representations that contribute to each level of task control (e.g., transparent networks in **Figure 5b**). That is, high "abstraction" can refer to task goals that are the most conceptually broad or temporally extended (see Badre & Nee, 2018), as well as representations that are the most coarse or categorical (Christophel et al., 2017; Freedman, Riesenhuber, Poggio, & Miller, 2001; Wutz, Loonis, Roy, Donoghue, & Miller, 2018), and coordination among these levels would facilitate context-appropriate behavior.

This organization would allow higher-order goals to be coordinated among the frontal network and adaptively communicated to task-relevant sub-networks (Figure 5c), rather than all regions and networks interacting (and potentially interfering) with one another. Those task-relevant sub-networks would then separately coordinate the composite aspects of each level of task control in parallel. This sort of nested hierarchy would confer several processing benefits: (1) It would allow the efficient selection of only the appropriate level of stimulus representation depending on the context, (2) several task-relevant computations could be carried out simultaneously in separate networks, and (3) representations at multiple levels of abstraction would provide redundancy to protect representations from interference at any one level (e.g., Gazzaley et al., 2004; Hwang et al., 2018; Kiyonaga, Dowd et al., 2017; Lorenc et al., 2015). For instance, when the overarching task goal is to "remember this face," it may be accompanied by subordinate processing rules like "if there is distraction, engage categorical representation regions" and further "if distraction is a face, inhibit sensory input." The activation of a categorical representation and inhibition of competing input would be unnecessary (and possibly costly) processes in other contexts; however, through the hierarchical control of network interactions, it can be engaged appropriately and simultaneously. Moreover, if stimulus information is represented at several levels of abstraction, a more coarse or categorical representation in higher regions may be able to bridge disruptions from distraction and reinstate sensory representations after distraction.

Although more rostral regions tend to represent more abstract information, there is not necessarily a one-to-one mapping among rostro-caudal cortical position, abstraction, and hierarchical role. For example, by measuring directed influences between brain regions using effective connectivity analyses (of fMRI activity), mid-lateral PFC was found to receive inputs from both anterior and posterior lateral PFC regions (Nee & D'Esposito, 2016). While more anterior frontal regions may represent the most temporally extended task goals, successful behavior depends on the coordination of those goals with more immediate context information and commands for action execution. This mid-lateral PFC region may therefore be crucial for integrating information across levels of representation and control, and across different task-relevant sub-networks. Indeed, mid-lateral PFC is commonly engaged during WM and is thought to carry flexible high-dimensional representations of many different task demands (e.g., Duncan, 2010; Rigotti et al., 2013). The region may serve as a nexus for coordinating communication among networks and may sit at the top of the hierarchy for integrating longer-term goals with immediate demands (Figure 5c). The hierarchical role of a region can therefore be understood not only by the type of information it represents but also its connectivity profile. That is, network connectivity patterns may also determine the hierarchical position of a brain region, with more diversely connected regions being well positioned to orchestrate integrative and higher-order control.

The previous section of the Element described WM maintenance as a network phenomenon across distributed brain regions, and it introduced two theoretical ideas about attentional control during WM: (1) that the involvement of individual brain regions within a network may shift depending on task demands and (2) that communication and coordination between networks for different functions are necessary to guide behavior. Here, we add that representations and task roles may be hierarchically organized both within and between these networks. WM activates distributed regions, and those activations may form hierarchically organized networks wherein the different regions (or nodes) make distinct contributions. A hierarchical flow of information within and between networks might allow the flexible implementation of representations depending on attentional and higher-order goals, also making WM robust to disruptions. Therefore, coordination among these hierarchically organized WM networks should promote successful behavior, and the final section of the Element will examine the connectivity properties that engender such flexible communication.

3.4 Network Segregation and Integration Provide a Framework for Flexible WM Maintenance

3.4.1 Network Modularity Relates to Performance

Graph theory is a branch of mathematics that can be applied to fMRI data, via measures of functional connectivity, to explore network topologies and nodal characteristics (Bullmore & Sporns, 2009; Rubinov & Sporns, 2010). By partitioning the brain into many nodes, then examining the strength and number of functional interactions between all nodes of the brain, these measures allow

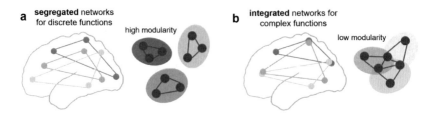

Figure 6 Network segregation and integration. (a) Functional connectivity can be used to define discrete sub-networks, or modules, within which nodes are strongly connected to each other. A high modularity system would display strong connections within sub-networks and weaker connections between sub-networks. (b) A low modularity system would display weaker exclusive connections within sub-networks and stronger connections between integrated sub-networks.

us to characterize large-scale brain organization. For instance, sets of nodes are organized into segregated network communities based on their connectivity affiliations, and these sub-networks or "modules" may perform discrete cognitive functions (Bertolero, Yeo, & D'Esposito, 2015). The extent of this segregation (i.e., modularity) in individuals, moreover, predicts the response to several cognitive training regimes (Arnemann et al., 2015; Baniqued et al., 2018; Gallen & D'Esposito, 2019; Gallen, Baniqued et al., 2016) and may relate to efficiency of function. As described above a hierarchical network configuration would be beneficial as it allows simultaneous processing at different levels of the hierarchy and imposes an organizational structure to coordinate context-appropriate behavior; this in turn might limit competition or interference between representations. A modular network architecture – wherein separate modules or sub-networks implement largely discrete functions – would confer similar benefits, isolating processing in one domain from potentially competing functions (**Figure 6a**). That is, component task elements may be efficiently carried out in parallel.

Here we describe how context-dependent connectivity properties, within and between brain networks, would form the basis for network-level attentional control during WM. Although modular network segregation may protect representations and processes from interference, an adaptive system would need to coordinate between these modules for complex tasks that engage multiple subfunctions. Accordingly, when a task relies on a discrete cognitive function, better behavior is associated with stronger network segregation (i.e., higher modularity, **Figure 6a**; Cohen & D'Esposito, 2016; Sadaghiani, Poline, Kleinschmidt, & D'Esposito, 2015). However, during a WM task that requires selective updating of content, maintenance of relevant representations, and selective inhibition of irrelevant representations, better performance is associated with increased integration and communication between sub-networks instead (e.g., **Figure 6b**; Cohen & D'Esposito, 2016; Cohen, Gallen, Jacobs, Lee, & D'Esposito, 2014; Gallen, Turner, Adnan, & D'Esposito, 2016). For instance, the cingulo-opercular and fronto-parietal intrinsic networks are thought to underlie task set maintenance and flexible updating, respectively. While these networks remain relatively segregated during a simple categorization task, they become more integrated when the task involves WM for the previous stimulus (Cohen et al., 2014). Moreover, the degree of integration between these intrinsic networks and a motor network relates to better WM accuracy. Thus, a segregated network architecture may be more adaptive for isolated cognitive processes that are most efficient to carry out locally. However, the flexible reconfiguration of that architecture may be necessary when behavior requires the integration of multiple levels of WM-relevant information – for instance, when overarching task goals need to be combined with context-specific rules for determining which representations to maintain and how to respond. The previous sections of this Element described how networks for WM representation might interact with networks for other functions to successfully guide action. We further propose that the capacity of networks to reconfigure into an optimal balance of segregation vs. integration will determine the ability to implement attentional control and resolve competition.

3.4.2 Diversely Connected Nodes May Coordinate the Large-Scale Connectivity Structure

In addition to quantifying the global network structure, connectivity patterns can be used to characterize the role of a particular region within a network – and within the whole brain architecture – based on the pattern of its network connections. For example, nodes can be characterized as provincial hubs that strengthen communication within a given network or as diversely affiliated connector hubs that facilitate the transfer of information between networks (**Figure 7a**). Connector hubs interact more diffusely with multiple other brain networks. Connectors increase their activity when greater numbers of cognitive functions are engaged (Bertolero et al., 2015) and correspond to the regions that are implicated in multiple cognitive demands (Bertolero, Yeo, & D'Esposito, 2017). Damage to these nodes is also associated with a breakdown of the whole-brain modular architecture, suggesting that they are responsible for maintaining the affiliations between regions (Gratton, Nomura, Pérez, & D'Esposito, 2012).

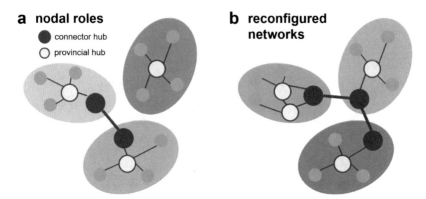

Figure 7 Nodal roles and network reconfiguration. (a) Provincial hubs (white circles) coordinate and communicate within a given network while connector hubs (large dark circles) communicate with other networks to facilitate the transfer of information between networks. (b) The roles of particular nodes and the degree of interaction between networks can change with task demands. For instance, a module may remain segregated to carry out a discrete task function (pink module), but will increase connectivity with modules for other functions to carry out complex and integrative functions.

These connector nodes would be well positioned to convey abstract attentional goals between networks (cf. Nee & D'Esposito, 2016), while provincial hubs might modify local activity dynamics within a sub-network. That is, the hierarchical position of a region in the control of behavior may relate to its nodal role in the large-scale connectivity architecture, with diversely connected hub nodes coordinating the integration across networks.

It is important to note that the network structure and node affiliations observed with these methods can be highly dependent on a wide variety of analytic choices, such as how finely the brain is parsed into nodes or what method is used to assign nodes to networks. That is, by saying that these methods can be used to characterize networks certainly does not mean that any given network characterization reflects the ground truth. Moreover, the network affiliation or nodal role of a region may change with task demands and cognitive state. In fact, that flexibility is the essence of the view we put forth here. That is, the task-dependent shifting in connectivity affiliations between WM network nodes (described in previous sections) suggests that nodal roles may adaptively shift in response to demands. This raises the intriguing possibility that different regions may sit at the top of the control hierarchy depending on which goals are currently paramount.

In sum, the connectivity profile of hub nodes – which correspond to regions that are regularly engaged by WM demands – relates to measures of network-level segregation and integration, which further relate to WM performance. These connectivity metrics may therefore index the capacity to adaptively reconfigure connectivity relationships for successful behavior. For instance, WM maintenance may be characterized by integration between domain-general attentional control sub-networks and perceptual processing sub-networks of the brain. Just as the appropriate level of hierarchical control (and representational abstraction) would depend on the current context, however, modules handling different levels of control would only integrate as necessary. When faced with competing attentional demands or perceptual input, those networks may reconfigure their affiliations to limit interference (**Figure 7b**). WM maintenance and perceptual attention processes may compete for the same attentional control networks at the systems level, while WM and perceptual content may compete in local sensory networks. These types of competition could be reduced by reconfiguration via long-range connector hubs and local provincial hubs, respectively. For instance, during WM dual-task processing, a high competition connectivity structure would be one wherein the nodes engaged for WM maintenance overlap with those for the intervening processing task. An adaptively reconfigured connectivity structure would reduce that competition by shifting the nodes and networks involved. In simple terms, therefore, controlling competition may rely on segregating competing networks.

4 Conclusions

Interactions between competing WM and perceptual content indicate that WM shares representational substrates and attentional control functions with perceptual attention. Top-down signals are exerted over these interactions via a multilevel network connectivity architecture, where activity in higher-order regions biases local activity and connectivity in sensory cortical representation regions. A distributed set of brain regions is therefore necessary to coordinate attentional control over challenges during WM maintenance (such as distraction and competition). WM maintenance and perceptual attention are subject to local competition for storage real estate, as well as systems-level competition for large-scale network processing space. WM and attentional networks may be characterized by a hierarchical organization of representation and control, which promotes the efficient performance of context-dependent behavior. Moreover, adaptive attentional control of WM may be implemented by network-level reconfiguration, orchestrated by diversely connected hub nodes. The degree of competition that manifests in behavior would therefore be determined by a combination of stimulus characteristics (i.e., degree of cortical overlap), task demands (i.e., degree of systems-level resource competition), the baseline organization of the network structure (i.e., modular network organization), and the capacity of the system to flexibly reconfigure (i.e., segregation vs. integration). Although the mechanisms underlying the hierarchical relationship between networks are currently unknown, nested hierarchical attentional control is likely supported by the connectivity structure within and between sub-networks of the brain. Thus, the principles of network segregation and integration, among multiple hierarchically organized sub-networks, may govern the flexible control over WM maintenance and perceptual attention.

In this Element we have introduced several new ideas about attentional control of WM: (1) WM competition may be managed by nested hierarchically organized networks; (2) the hierarchical role of a region (and the kind of information that is represented there) may be related to its network connectivity properties, and those may shift based on context; and (3) such shifting of nodal roles likely represents a network-level reconfiguration that manages competition for storage and processing space. Yet these ideas spark several outstanding questions. We have theorized that network connectivity properties might determine a region's hierarchical role, but it is currently unclear whether nodal connectivity characteristics (e.g., within- or between-network connectedness of a region) are also organized along a rostro-caudal cortical gradient, or whether these network connectivity properties relate to the representational abstraction of a region. Moreover, we have suggested that diversely connected hub nodes may sit atop the control hierarchy, but it is unknown by what means these regions influence information processing. Do these hub nodes bear unique anatomical or functional properties that facilitate this role, or are they merely shared among many networks and functions? We have also proposed that these nodes coordinate the whole-brain balance between network segregation and integration, but the relationship between network reconfiguration and behavioral indices of interference and control have yet to be tested. Finally, while there are many parallels between WM maintenance and perceptual attention, a self-evident property of WM that distinguishes it from externally oriented attention is that WM content must be endogenously maintained when the perceptual input is no longer present to evoke the representation. What features distinguish between the representations and top-down modulatory processes for WM vs. perceptual attention? For instance, emerging theories suggest that perceptual vs. WM content may be represented in shared cortical tissue but via distinct layers of that tissue

(Rademaker et al., 2019; van Kerkoerle et al., 2017), allowing us to process both simultaneously. Exciting advances in high-field MRI and multivariate analyses methods will enable us to address these questions, thereby gaining traction on the processes that underlie our remarkable – but sometimes fragile – ability to juggle internal thoughts and goals with immediate demands in the environment.

References

Albouy, P., Weiss, A., Baillet, S., & Zatorre, R. J. (2017). Selective entrainment of theta oscillations in the dorsal stream causally enhances auditory working memory performance. *Neuron, 94*(1), 193–206.e5. https://doi.org/10.1016/j.neuron.2017.03.015

Arnemann, K. L., Chen, A. J.-W., Novakovic-Agopian, T., Gratton, C., Nomura, E. M., & D'Esposito, M. (2015). Functional brain network modularity predicts response to cognitive training after brain injury. *Neurology, 84*(15), 1568–1574. https://doi.org/10.1212/WNL.0000000000001476

Awh, E., & Jonides, J. (2001). Overlapping mechanisms of attention and spatial working memory. *Trends in Cognitive Sciences, 5*(3), 119–126.

Baddeley, A. (2003). Working memory: Looking back and looking forward. *Nature Reviews Neuroscience, 4*(10), 829–839.

Baddeley, A. D., & Hitch, G. J. (2018). The phonological loop as a buffer store: An update. *Cortex.* https://doi.org/10.1016/j.cortex.2018.05.015

Badre, D., & D'Esposito, M. (2007). Functional magnetic resonance imaging evidence for a hierarchical organization of the prefrontal cortex. *Journal of Cognitive Neuroscience, 19*(12), 2082–2099. https://doi.org/10.1162/jocn.2007.19.12.2082

Badre, D., & D'esposito, M. (2009). Is the rostro-caudal axis of the frontal lobe hierarchical?. *Nature Reviews Neuroscience, 10*(9), 659–669.

Badre, D., Hoffman, J., Cooney, J. W., & D'Esposito, M. (2009). Hierarchical cognitive control deficits following damage to the human frontal lobe. *Nature Neuroscience, 12*(4), 515–522. https://doi.org/10.1038/nn.2277

Badre, D., & Nee, D. E. (2018). Frontal cortex and the hierarchical control of behavior. *Trends in Cognitive Sciences, 22*(2), 170–188. https://doi.org/10.1016/j.tics.2017.11.005

Bae, G.-Y., & Luck, S. J. (2018). Dissociable decoding of spatial attention and working memory from EEG oscillations and sustained potentials. *Journal of Neuroscience, 38*(2), 409–422. https://doi.org/10.1523/JNEUROSCI.2860–17.2017

Baniqued, P. L., Gallen, C. L., Voss, M. W., Burzynska, A. Z., Wong, C. N., Cooke, G. E., . . . D'Esposito, M. (2018). Brain network modularity predicts exercise-related executive function gains in older adults. *Frontiers in Aging Neuroscience, 9.* https://doi.org/10.3389/fnagi.2017.00426

Barbosa, J., Stein, H., Martinez, R. L., Galan-Gadea, A., Li, S., Dalmau, J., . . . & Compte, A. (2020). Interplay between persistent activity and activity-silent dynamics in the prefrontal cortex underlies serial biases in working memory. *Nature Neuroscience*, 23, 1016–1024.

Barrouillet, P., Portrat, S., & Camos, V. (2011). On the law relating processing to storage in working memory. *Psychological Review, 118*(2), 175.

Behrmann, M., & Plaut, D. C. (2013). Distributed circuits, not circumscribed centers, mediate visual recognition. *Trends in Cognitive Sciences, 17*(5), 210–219. https://doi.org/10.1016/j.tics.2013.03.007

Bergmann, J., Genç, E., Kohler, A., Singer, W., & Pearson, J. (2016). Neural anatomy of primary visual cortex limits visual working memory. *Cerebral Cortex, 26*(1), 43–50. https://doi.org/10.1093/cercor/bhu168

Bertolero, M. A., Yeo, B. T., & D'Esposito, M. (2015). The modular and integrative functional architecture of the human brain. *Proceedings of the National Academy of Sciences, 112*(49), E6798–E6807.

(2017). The diverse club. *Nature Communications, 8*(1), 1–11.

Bettencourt, K. C., & Xu, Y. (2016). Decoding the content of visual short-term memory under distraction in occipital and parietal areas. *Nature Neuroscience, 19*(1), 150–157. https://doi.org/10.1038/nn.4174

Bliss, D. P., & D'Esposito, M. (2017). Synaptic augmentation in a cortical circuit model reproduces serial dependence in visual working memory. *PLOS ONE, 12*(12), e0188927. https://doi.org/10.1371/journal.pone.0188927

Bliss, D. P., Sun, J. J., & D'Esposito, M. (2017). Serial dependence is absent at the time of perception but increases in visual working memory. *Scientific Reports, 7*. https://doi.org/10.1038/s41598-017–15199-7

Bullmore, E., & Sporns, O. (2009). Complex brain networks: Graph theoretical analysis of structural and functional systems. *Nature Reviews Neuroscience, 10*(3), 186–198. https://doi.org/10.1038/nrn2575

Buschman, T. J., & Miller, E. K. (2007). Top-down versus bottom-up control of attention in the prefrontal and posterior parietal cortices. *Science, 315* (5820), 1860–1862. https://doi.org/10.1126/science.1138071

Buzsáki, G., & Draguhn, A. (2004). Neuronal oscillations in cortical networks. *Science, 304*(5679), 1926–1929. https://doi.org/10.1126/science.1099745

Carlisle, N. B., & Woodman, G. F. (2011). Automatic and strategic effects in the guidance of attention by working memory representations. *Acta Psychologica, 137*(2), 217–225.

Chen, K., Ye, Y., Xie, J., Xia, T., & Mo, L. (2017). Working memory operates over the same representations as attention. *PLOS ONE, 12*(6), e0179382.

Choi, E. Y., Drayna, G. K., & Badre, D. (2018). Evidence for a functional hierarchy of association networks. *Journal of Cognitive Neuroscience, 30*(5), 722–736.

Christophel, T. B., Hebart, M. N., & Haynes, J. D. (2012). Decoding the contents of visual short-term memory from human visual and parietal cortex. *Journal of Neuroscience, 32*(38), 12983–12989.

Christophel, T. B., Iamshchinina, P., Yan, C., Allefeld, C., & Haynes, J.-D. (2018). Cortical specialization for attended versus unattended working memory. *Nature Neuroscience,* 21, 494–496. https://doi.org/10.1038/s41593-018-0094-4

Christophel, T. B., Klink, P. C., Spitzer, B., Roelfsema, P. R., & Haynes, J.-D. (2017). The distributed nature of working memory. *Trends in Cognitive Sciences, 21*(2), 111–124. https://doi.org/10.1016/j.tics.2016.12.007

Chun, M. M. (2011). Visual working memory as visual attention sustained internally over time. *Neuropsychologia, 49*(6), 1407–1409. https://doi.org/10.1016/j.neuropsychologia.2011.01.029

Chun, M. M., & Johnson, M. K. (2011). Memory: Enduring traces of perceptual and reflective attention. *Neuron, 72*(4), 520–535. https://doi.org/10.1016/j.neuron.2011.10.026

Cohen, J. D., Dunbar, K., & McClelland, J. L. (1990). On the control of automatic processes: A parallel distributed processing account of the Stroop effect. *Psychological Review, 97*(3), 332–361. https://doi.org/10.1037/0033-295X.97.3.332

Cohen, J. R., & D'Esposito, M. (2016). The segregation and integration of distinct brain networks and their relationship to cognition. *Journal of Neuroscience, 36*(48), 12083–12094. https://doi.org/10.1523/JNEUROSCI.2965-15.2016

Cohen, J. R., Gallen, C. L., Jacobs, E. G., Lee, T. G., & D'Esposito, M. (2014). Quantifying the reconfiguration of intrinsic networks during working memory. *PLOS ONE, 9*(9), e106636. https://doi.org/10.1371/journal.pone.0106636

Constantinidis, C., & Klingberg, T. (2016). The neuroscience of working memory capacity and training. *Nature Reviews Neuroscience, 17*(7), 438–449. https://doi.org/10.1038/nrn.2016.43

Curtis, C. E., & D'Esposito, M. (2003). Persistent activity in the prefrontal cortex during working memory. *Trends in Cognitive Sciences, 7*(9), 415–423. https://doi.org/10.1016/S1364-6613(03)00197-9

Cutzu, F., & Tsotsos, J. K. (2003). The selective tuning model of attention: Psychophysical evidence for a suppressive annulus around an attended item. *Vision Research, 43*(2), 205–219. https://doi.org/10.1016/S0042-6989(02)00491-1

David, S. V., Hayden, B. Y., Mazer, J. A., & Gallant, J. L. (2008). Attention to stimulus features shifts spectral tuning of V4 neurons during natural vision. *Neuron*, *59*(3), 509–521. https://doi.org/10.1016/j.neuron.2008.07.001

Derrfuss, J., Ekman, M., Hanke, M., Tittgemeyer, M., & Fiebach, C. J. (2017). Distractor-resistant short-term memory is supported by transient changes in neural stimulus representations. *Journal of Cognitive Neuroscience*, 29 (9), 1547–1565. https://doi.org/10.1162/jocn_a_01141

Desimone, R., & Duncan, J. (1995). Neural mechanisms of selective visual attention. *Annual Review of Neuroscience*, *18*(1), 193–222. https://doi.org /10.1146/annurev.ne.18.030195.001205

D'Esposito, M. (2007). From cognitive to neural models of working memory. *Philosophical Transactions of the Royal Society B: Biological Sciences*, *362*(1481), 761–772.

D'Esposito, M., Aguirre, G. K., Zarahn, E., Ballard, D., Shin, R. K., & Lease, J. (1998). Functional MRI studies of spatial and nonspatial working memory. *Cognitive Brain Research*, *7*(1), 1–13. https://doi.org/10.1016/S0926-6410(98)00004–4

D'Esposito, M., Ballard, D., Aguirre, G. K., & Zarahn, E. (1998). Human prefrontal cortex is not specific for working memory: A functional MRI study. *NeuroImage*, *8*(3), 274–282. https://doi.org/10.1006/nimg.1998.0364

D'Esposito, M., Cooney, J. W., Gazzaley, A., Gibbs, S. E. B., & Postle, B. R. (2006). Is the prefrontal cortex necessary for delay task performance? Evidence from lesion and FMRI data. *Journal of the International Neuropsychological Society: JINS*, *12*(2), 248–260. https://doi.org/10 .1017/S1355617706060322

D'Esposito, M., & Grossman, M. (1996). The physiological basis of executive function and working memory. *The Neuroscientist*, *2*(6), 345–352. https:// doi.org/10.1177/107385849600200612

D'Esposito, M., & Postle, B. R. (1999). The dependence of span and delayed-response performance on prefrontal cortex. *Neuropsychologia*, *37*(11), 1303–1315. https://doi.org/10.1016/S0028-3932(99)00021–4

(2015). The cognitive neuroscience of working memory. *Annual Review of Psychology*, *66*(1), 115–142. https://doi.org/10.1146/annurev-psych -010814–015031

D'Esposito, M., Postle, B. R., Ballard, D., & Lease, J. (1999). Maintenance versus manipulation of information held in working memory: An event-related fMRI study. *Brain and Cognition*, *41*(1), 66–86. https://doi .org/10.1006/brcg.1999.1096

D'Esposito, M., Postle, B. R., Jonides, J., & Smith, E. E. (1999). The neural substrate and temporal dynamics of interference effects in working memory as revealed by event-related functional MRI. *Proceedings of the National Academy of Sciences*, *96*(13), 7514–7519. https://doi.org/10.1073/pnas.96.13.7514

de Vries, I. E., Slagter, H. A., & Olivers, C. N. (2020). Oscillatory control over representational states in working memory. *Trends in Cognitive Sciences*, *24*(2), 150–162.

Dowd, E. W., Kiyonaga, A., Beck, J. M., & Egner, T. (2015). Quality and accessibility of visual working memory during cognitive control of attentional guidance: A Bayesian model comparison approach. *Visual Cognition*, 23(3), 337–356. https://doi.org/10.1080/13506285.2014.1003631

Dowd, E. W., Kiyonaga, A., Egner, T., & Mitroff, S. R. (2015). Attentional guidance by working memory differs by paradigm: An individual-differences approach. *Attention, Perception, & Psychophysics*, *77*(3), 704–712. https://doi.org/10.3758/s13414-015-0847-z

Druzgal, T. J., & D'Esposito, M. (2001). Activity in fusiform face area modulated as a function of working memory. *Cognitive Brain Research*, *10*(3), 355–364. https://doi.org/10.1016/S0926-6410(00)00056-2

Duncan, J. (2010). The multiple-demand (MD) system of the primate brain: mental programs for intelligent behaviour. *Trends in cognitive sciences*, *14*(4), 172–179.

Emrich, S. M., & Ferber, S. (2012). Competition increases binding errors in visual working memory. *Journal of Vision*, *12*(4), 12–12. https://doi.org/10.1167/12.4.12

Eriksson, J., Vogel, E. K., Lansner, A., Bergström, F., & Nyberg, L. (2015). Neurocognitive architecture of working memory. *Neuron*, *88*(1), 33–46. https://doi.org/10.1016/j.neuron.2015.09.020

Ester, E. F., Anderson, D. E., Serences, J. T., & Awh, E. (2013). A neural measure of precision in visual working memory. *Journal of Cognitive Neuroscience*, *25*(5), 754–761. https://doi.org/10.1162/jocn_a_00357

Ester, E. F., Sprague, T. C., & Serences, J. T. (2015). Parietal and frontal cortex encode stimulus-specific mnemonic representations during visual working memory. *Neuron*, *87*(4), 893–905.

Feldmann-Wüstefeld, T., Vogel, E. K., & Awh, E. (2018). Contralateral delay activity indexes working memory storage, not the current focus of spatial attention. *Journal of Cognitive Neuroscience*, *30*(8), 1185–1196.

Feredoes, E., Heinen, K., Weiskopf, N., Ruff, C., & Driver, J. (2011). Causal evidence for frontal involvement in memory target maintenance by posterior brain areas during distracter interference of visual working memory.

Proceedings of the National Academy of Sciences, *108*(42), 17510–17515. https://doi.org/10.1073/pnas.1106439108

Fiebach, C. J., Rissman, J., & D'Esposito, M. (2006). Modulation of infero-temporal cortex activation during verbal working memory maintenance. *Neuron*, *51*(2), 251–261. https://doi.org/10.1016/j.neuron.2006.06.007

Fischer, J., & Whitney, D. (2014). Serial dependence in visual perception. *Nature Neuroscience*, *17*(5), 738–743.

Franconeri, S. L., Alvarez, G. A., & Cavanagh, P. (2013). Flexible cognitive resources: Competitive content maps for attention and memory. *Trends in Cognitive Sciences*, *17*(3), 134–141. https://doi.org/10.1016/j.tics.2013.01.010

Franconeri, S. L., Jonathan, S. V., & Scimeca, J. M. (2010). Tracking multiple objects is limited only by object spacing, not by speed, time, or capacity. *Psychological Science*, *21*(7), 920–925. https://doi.org/10.1177/0956797610373935

Freedman, D. J., Riesenhuber, M., Poggio, T., & Miller, E. K. (2001). Categorical representation of visual stimuli in the primate prefrontal cortex. *Science*, *291*(5502), 312–316. https://doi.org/10.1126/science.291.5502.312

Friedman-Hill, S. R., Robertson, L. C., Desimone, R., & Ungerleider, L. G. (2003). Posterior parietal cortex and the filtering of distractors. *Proceedings of the National Academy of Sciences*, *100*(7), 4263–4268. https://doi.org/10.1073/pnas.0730772100

Fries, P. (2015). Rhythms for cognition: communication through coherence. *Neuron*, *88*(1), 220–235. https://doi.org/10.1016/j.neuron.2015.09.034

Gallen, C. L., Baniqued, P. L., Chapman, S. B., Aslan, S., Keebler, M., Didehbani, N., & D'Esposito, M. (2016). Modular brain network organization predicts response to cognitive training in older adults. *PLOS ONE*, *11*(12), e0169015. https://doi.org/10.1371/journal.pone.0169015

Gallen, C. L., & D'Esposito, M. (2019). Brain modularity: A biomarker of intervention-related plasticity. *Trends in Cognitive Sciences*, *23*, 293–304. https://doi.org/10.1016/j.tics.2019.01.014

Gallen, C. L., Turner, G. R., Adnan, A., & D'Esposito, M. (2016). Reconfiguration of brain network architecture to support executive control in aging. *Neurobiology of Aging*, *44*, 42–52. https://doi.org/10.1016/j.neurobiolaging.2016.04.003

Gayet, S., Guggenmos, M., Christophel, T. B., Haynes, J.-D., Paffen, C. L. E., der Stigchel, S. V., & Sterzer, P. (2017). Visual working memory enhances the neural response to matching visual input. *Journal of Neuroscience*, *37*(28), 6638–6647. https://doi.org/10.1523/JNEUROSCI.3418–16.2017

Gayet, S., Paffen, C. L. E., & der Stigchel, S. V. (2018). Visual working memory storage recruits sensory processing areas. *Trends in Cognitive Sciences*, *22* (3), 189–190. https://doi.org/10.1016/j.tics.2017.09.011

Gazzaley, A., & Nobre, A. C. (2012). Top-down modulation: Bridging selective attention and working memory. *Trends in Cognitive Sciences*, *16*(2), 129–135. https://doi.org/10.1016/j.tics.2011.11.014

Gazzaley, A., Rissman, J., Cooney, J., Rutman, A., Seibert, T., Clapp, W., & D'Esposito, M. (2007). Functional interactions between prefrontal and visual association cortex contribute to top-down modulation of visual processing. *Cerebral Cortex*, *17*(suppl_1), i125–i135. https://doi.org/10 .1093/cercor/bhm113

Gazzaley, A., Rissman, J., & D'Esposito, M. (2004). Functional connectivity during working memory maintenance. *Cognitive, Affective, & Behavioral Neuroscience*, *4*(4), 580–599. https://doi.org/10.3758/CABN.4.4.580

Gratton, C., Nomura, E. M., Pérez, F., & D'Esposito, M. (2012). Focal brain lesions to critical locations cause widespread disruption of the modular organization of the brain. *Journal of Cognitive Neuroscience*, *24*(6), 1275–1285. https://doi.org/10.1162/jocn_a_00222

Griffin, I. C., & Nobre, A. C. (2003). Orienting attention to locations in internal representations. *Journal of Cognitive Neuroscience*, *15*(8), 1176–1194. https://doi.org/10.1162/089892903322598139

Hakim, N., Adam, K. C., Gunseli, E., Awh, E., & Vogel, E. K. (2019). Dissecting the neural focus of attention reveals distinct processes for spatial attention and object-based storage in visual working memory. *Psychological Science*, *30*(4), 526–540.

Hakim, N., Feldmann-Wüstefeld, T., Awh, E., & Vogel, E. K. (2020). Perturbing neural representations of working memory with task-irrelevant interruption. *Journal of Cognitive Neuroscience*, *32*(3), 558–569.

Harrison, S. A., & Tong, F. (2009). Decoding reveals the contents of visual working memory in early visual areas. *Nature*, *458*(7238), 632–635. https://doi.org/10.1038/nature07832

Harrison, W. J., & Bays, P. M. (2018). Visual working memory is independent of the cortical spacing between memoranda. *Journal of Neuroscience*, *38* (12), 3116–3123. https://doi.org/10.1523/JNEUROSCI.2645-17.2017

Hillyard, S. A., Vogel, E. K., & Luck, S. J. (1998). Sensory gain control (amplification) as a mechanism of selective attention: Electrophysiological and neuroimaging evidence. *Philosophical Transactions of the Royal Society of London B: Biological Sciences*, *353*(1373), 1257–1270. https://doi.org/10 .1098/rstb.1998.0281

Hollingworth, A., Matsukura, M., & Luck, S. J. (2013). Visual working memory modulates low-level saccade target selection: Evidence from rapidly generated saccades in the global effect paradigm. *Journal of Vision*, *13*(13), 4–4. https://doi.org/10.1167/13.13.4

Hollingworth, A., & Maxcey-Richard, A. M. (2012). Selective maintenance in visual working memory does not require sustained visual attention. *Journal of Experimental Psychology. Human Perception and Performance*, *39*(4), 1047–1058. https://doi.org/10.1037/a0030238

Hopf, J.-M., Boehler, C. N., Luck, S. J., Tsotsos, J. K., Heinze, H.-J., & Schoenfeld, M. A. (2006). Direct neurophysiological evidence for spatial suppression surrounding the focus of attention in vision. *Proceedings of the National Academy of Sciences of the United States of America*, *103*(4), 1053–1058. https://doi.org/10.1073/pnas.0507746103

Hwang, K., Shine, J. M., & D'Esposito, M. (2018). Frontoparietal activity interacts with task-evoked changes in functional connectivity. *Cerebral Cortex*, *29*(2) 802–813. https://doi.org/10.1093/cercor/bhy011

Jacob, S. N., & Nieder, A. (2014). Complementary roles for primate frontal and parietal cortex in guarding working memory from distractor stimuli. *Neuron*, *83*(1), 226–237. https://doi.org/10.1016/j.neuron.2014.05.009

Jacobsen, C. F. (1935). Functions of frontal association area in primates. *Archives of Neurology & Psychiatry*, *33*(3), 558–569. https://doi.org/10.1001/archneurpsyc.1935.02250150108009

Jha, A. P., & Kiyonaga, A. (2010). Working-memory-triggered dynamic adjustments in cognitive control. *Journal of Experimental Psychology. Learning, Memory, and Cognition*, *36*(4), 1036–1042. https://doi.org/10.1037/a0019337

John-Saaltink, E. S., Kok, P., Lau, H. C., & Lange, F. P. de. (2016). Serial dependence in perceptual decisions is reflected in activity patterns in primary visual cortex. *Journal of Neuroscience*, *36*(23), 6186–6192. https://doi.org/10.1523/JNEUROSCI.4390–15.2016

Johnson, M. R., Higgins, J. A., Norman, K. A., Sederberg, P. B., Smith, T. A., & Johnson, M. K. (2013). Foraging for thought: An inhibition-of-return-like effect resulting from directing attention within working memory. *Psychological Science*, *24*(7), 1104–1112. https://doi.org/10.1177/0956797612466414

Jonides, J., & Nee, D. E. (2006). Brain mechanisms of proactive interference in working memory. *Neuroscience*, *139*(1), 181–193. https://doi.org/10.1016/j.neuroscience.2005.06.042

Kim, S. Y., Kim, M. S., & Chun, M. M. (2005). Concurrent working memory load can reduce distraction. *Proceedings of the National Academy of Sciences of the United States of America*, *102*(45), 16524.

Kiyonaga, A., Dowd, E. W., & Egner, T. (2017). Neural representation of working memory content is modulated by visual attentional demand. *Journal of Cognitive Neuroscience*, *29*(12), 2011–2024. https://doi.org/10.1162/jocn_a_01174

Kiyonaga, A., & Egner, T. (2013). Working memory as internal attention: Toward an integrative account of internal and external selection processes. *Psychonomic Bulletin & Review*, *20*(2), 228–242. https://doi.org/10.3758/s13423-012–0359-y

(2014a). Resource-sharing between internal maintenance and external selection modulates attentional capture by working memory content. *Frontiers in Human Neuroscience*, *8*, 670. https://doi.org/10.3389/fnhum.2014.00670

(2014b). The working memory Stroop effect when internal representations clash with external stimuli. *Psychological Science*, *25*(8), 1619–1629. https://doi.org/10.1177/0956797614536739

(2016). Center-surround inhibition in working memory. *Current Biology*, *26*(1), 64–68. https://doi.org/10.1016/j.cub.2015.11.013

Kiyonaga, A., Egner, T., & Soto, D. (2012). Cognitive control over working memory biases of selection. *Psychonomic Bulletin & Review*, *19*(4), 639–646. https://doi.org/10.3758/s13423-012–0253-7

Kiyonaga, A., Korb, F. M., Lucas, J., Soto, D., & Egner, T. (2014). Dissociable causal roles for left and right parietal cortex in controlling attentional biases from the contents of working memory. *NeuroImage*, *100*, 200–205. https://doi.org/10.1016/j.neuroimage.2014.06.019

Kiyonaga, A., Scimeca, J. M., Bliss, D. P., & Whitney, D. (2017). Serial dependence across perception, attention, and memory. *Trends in Cognitive Sciences*, *21*(7), 493–497. https://doi.org/10.1016/j.tics.2017.04.011

Knight, R. T., Richard Staines, W., Swick, D., & Chao, L. L. (1999). Prefrontal cortex regulates inhibition and excitation in distributed neural networks. *Acta Psychologica*, *101*(2–3), 159–178. https://doi.org/10.1016/S0001-6918(99)00004–9

Lara, A. H., & Wallis, J. D. (2015). The role of prefrontal cortex in working memory: A mini review. *Frontiers in Systems Neuroscience*, 173. https://doi.org/10.3389/fnsys.2015.00173

LaRocque, J. J., Lewis-Peacock, J. A., & Postle, B. R. (2014). Multiple neural states of representation in short-term memory? It's a matter of attention. *Frontiers in Human Neuroscience*, *8*. https://doi.org/10.3389/fnhum.2014.00005

Leavitt, M. L., Mendoza-Halliday, D., & Martinez-Trujillo, J. C. (2017). Sustained activity encoding working memories: Not fully distributed. *Trends in Neurosciences, 40*(6), 328–346. https://doi.org/10.1016/j.tins.2017.04.004

Lee, T. G., & D'Esposito, M. (2012). The dynamic nature of top-down signals originating from prefrontal cortex: A combined fMRI–TMS study. *The Journal of Neuroscience, 32*(44), 15458–15466. https://doi.org/10.1523 /JNEUROSCI.0627–12.2012

Lepsien, J., Griffin, I. C., Devlin, J. T., & Nobre, A. C. (2005). Directing spatial attention in mental representations: Interactions between attentional orienting and working-memory load. *NeuroImage, 26*(3), 733–743. https://doi.org/10.1016/j.neuroimage.2005.02.026

Lepsien, J., & Nobre, A. C. (2006). Cognitive control of attention in the human brain: Insights from orienting attention to mental representations. *Brain Research, 1105*(1), 20–31. https://doi.org/10.1016/j.brainres.2006.03.033

(2007). Attentional modulation of object representations in working memory. *Cerebral Cortex, 17*(9), 2072–2083. https://doi.org/10.1093/cer cor/bhl116

Lewis-Peacock, J. A., Drysdale, A. T., & Postle, B. R. (2014). Neural evidence for the flexible control of mental representations. *Cerebral Cortex, 25*(10), 3303–3313. https://doi.org/10.1093/cercor/bhu130

Lorenc, E. S., Lee, T. G., Chen, A. J.-W., & D'Esposito, M. (2015). The effect of disruption of prefrontal cortical function with transcranial magnetic stimulation on visual working memory. *Frontiers in Systems Neuroscience, 9.* https://doi.org/10.3389/fnsys.2015.00169

Lorenc, E. S., Sreenivasan, K. K., Nee, D. E., Vandenbroucke, A. R. E., & D'Esposito, M. (2018). Flexible coding of visual working memory representations during distraction. *Journal of Neuroscience, 38*(23), 5267–5276. https://doi.org/10.1523/JNEUROSCI.3061–17.2018

Lorenc, E. S., Vandenbroucke, A. R., Nee, D. E., de Lange, F. P., & D'Esposito, M. (2020). Dissociable neural mechanisms underlie currently-relevant, future-relevant, and discarded working memory representations. *Scientific Reports, 10*(1), 1–17.

MacLeod, C. M. (1991). Half a century of research on the Stroop effect: An integrative review. *Psychological Bulletin, 109*(2), 163–203. https://doi .org/10.1037/0033–2909.109.2.163

Magen, H., Emmanouil, T.-A., McMains, S. A., Kastner, S., & Treisman, A. (2009). Attentional demands predict short-term memory load response in posterior parietal cortex. *Neuropsychologia, 47*(8–9), 1790–1798. https:// doi.org/10.1016/j.neuropsychologia.2009.02.015

Magnussen, S., & Greenlee, M. W. (1992). Retention and disruption of motion information in visual short-term memory. *Journal of Experimental Psychology. Learning, Memory, and Cognition, 18*(1), 151–156.

Magnussen, S., Greenlee, M. W., Asplund, R., & Dyrnes, S. (1991). Stimulus-specific mechanisms of visual short-term memory. *Vision Research, 31*(7), 1213–1219. https://doi.org/10.1016/0042–6989(91)90046–8

Mallett, R., & Lewis-Peacock, J. A. (2018). Behavioral decoding of working memory items inside and outside the focus of attention. *Annals of the New York Academy of Sciences, 1424*(1), 256–267. https://doi.org/10.1111/nyas.13647

Mallett, R., Mummaneni, A., & Lewis-Peacock, J. A. (2020). Distraction biases working memory for faces. *Psychonomic Bulletin & Review*, 1–7.

Malmo, R. B. (1942). Interference factors in delayed response in monkeys after removal of frontal lobes. *Journal of Neurophysiology, 5*(4), 295–308.

McNab, F., & Klingberg, T. (2008). Prefrontal cortex and basal ganglia control access to working memory. *Nature Neuroscience, 11*(1), 103–107. https://doi.org/10.1038/nn2024

Mendoza-Halliday, D., & Martinez-Trujillo, J. C. (2017). Neuronal population coding of perceived and memorized visual features in the lateral prefrontal cortex. *Nature Communications, 8*, 15471. https://doi.org/10.1038/ncomms15471

Merrikhi, Y., Clark, K., Albarran, E., Parsa, M., Zirnsak, M., Moore, T., & Noudoost, B. (2017). Spatial working memory alters the efficacy of input to visual cortex. *Nature Communications, 8*, 15041. https://doi.org/10.1038/ncomms15041

Miller, B. T., & D'Esposito, M. (2005). Searching for "the top" in top-down control. *Neuron, 48*(4), 535–538. https://doi.org/10.1016/j.neuron.2005.11.002

Miller, E. K., & Cohen, J. D. (2001). An integrative theory of prefrontal cortex function. *Annual review of neuroscience, 24*(1), 167–202.

Miller, J. A., Kiyonaga, A., Ivry, R. B., & D'Esposito, M. (in press). Prioritized working memory content biases ongoing action. Journal of Experimental Psychology: Human Perception and Performance. http://dx.doi.org/10.1037/xhp0000868

Moran, J., & Desimone, R. (1985). Selective attention gates visual processing in the extrastriate cortex. *Science, 229*(4715), 782–784.

Myers, N. E., Stokes, M. G., & Nobre, A. C. (2017). Prioritizing information during working memory: Beyond sustained internal attention. *Trends in Cognitive Sciences, 21*(6), 449–461. https://doi.org/10.1016/j.tics.2017.03.010

Nassi, J. J., Lomber, S. G., & Born, R. T. (2013). Corticocortical feedback contributes to surround suppression in V1 of the alert primate. *Journal of Neuroscience*, *33*(19), 8504–8517. https://doi.org/10.1523/JNEUROSCI.5124–12.2013

Nee, D. E., & D'Esposito, M. (2016). The hierarchical organization of the lateral prefrontal cortex. *ELife*, *5*. https://doi.org/10.7554/eLife.12112

Nee, D. E., & Jonides, J. (2008). Neural correlates of access to short-term memory. *Proceedings of the National Academy of Sciences*, *105*(37), 14228–14233. https://doi.org/10.1073/pnas.0802081105

(2009). Common and distinct neural correlates of perceptual and memorial selection. *NeuroImage*, *45*(3), 963–975. https://doi.org/10.1016/j.neuroimage.2009.01.005

Nelissen, N., Stokes, M., Nobre, A. C., & Rushworth, M. F. S. (2013). Frontal and parietal cortical interactions with distributed visual representations during selective attention and action selection. *The Journal of Neuroscience*, *33*(42), 16443–16458. https://doi.org/10.1523/JNEUROSCI.2625–13.2013

Nemes, V. A., Parry, N. R. A., Whitaker, D., & McKeefry, D. J. (2012). The retention and disruption of color information in human short-term visual memory. *Journal of Vision*, *12*(1), 26–26. https://doi.org/10.1167/12.1.26

Nobre, A. C., Coull, J. T., Maquet, P., Frith, C. D., Vandenberghe, R., & Mesulam, M. M. (2004). Orienting attention to locations in perceptual versus mental representations. *Journal of Cognitive Neuroscience*, *16*(3), 363–373. https://doi.org/10.1162/089892904322926700

Norman, K. A., Polyn, S. M., Detre, G. J., & Haxby, J. V. (2006). Beyond mind-reading: Multi-voxel pattern analysis of fMRI data. *Trends in Cognitive Sciences*, *10*(9), 424–430. https://doi.org/10.1016/j.tics.2006.07.005

Oberauer, K., & Lin, H.-Y. (2017). An interference model of visual working memory. *Psychological Review*, *124*(1), 21–59. https://doi.org/10.1037/rev0000044

O'Craven, K. M., Downing, P. E., & Kanwisher, N. (1999). fMRI evidence for objects as the units of attentional selection. *Nature*, *401*(6753), 584–587. https://doi.org/10.1038/44134

Olivers, C. N. L., Peters, J., Houtkamp, R., & Roelfsema, P. R. (2011). Different states in visual working memory: When it guides attention and when it does not. *Trends in Cognitive Sciences*, *15*(7). https://doi.org/10.1016/j.tics.2011.05.004

Oztekin, I., & Badre, D. (2011). Distributed patterns of brain activity that lead to forgetting. *Frontiers in Human Neuroscience*, *5*. https://doi.org/10.3389/fnhum.2011.00086

Pan, Y., Han, Y., & Zuo, W. (2019). The color-word Stroop effect driven by working memory maintenance. *Attention, Perception, & Psychophysics*, *81*(8), 2722–2731.

Papadimitriou, C., White, R. L., & Snyder, L. H. (2016). Ghosts in the machine II: Neural correlates of memory interference from the previous trial. *Cerebral Cortex*, *27*(4), 2513–2527. https://doi.org/10.1093/cercor/bhw106

Pasternak, T., & Greenlee, M. W. (2005). Working memory in primate sensory systems. *Nature Reviews Neuroscience*, *6*(2), 97–107. https://doi.org/10.1038/nrn1603

Pelli, D. G., & Tillman, K. A. (2008). The uncrowded window of object recognition. *Nature Neuroscience*, *11*(10), 1129–1135. https://doi.org/10.1038/nn.2187

Pertzov, Y., Manohar, S., & Husain, M. (2017). rapid forgetting results from competition over time between items in visual working memory. *Journal of Experimental Psychology. Learning, Memory, and Cognition*, *43*(4), 528–536. https://doi.org/10.1037/xlm0000328

Pessoa, L. (2012). Beyond brain regions: Network perspective of cognition–emotion interactions. *Behavioral and Brain Sciences*, *35*(3), 158–159. https://doi.org/10.1017/S0140525X11001567

Posner, M. I. (1980). Orienting of attention. *Quarterly Journal of Experimental Psychology*, *32*(1), 3–25. https://doi.org/10.1080/00335558008248231

Posner, M. I., & Snyder, C. R. R. (1975). Facilitation and inhibition in the processing of signals. *Attention and Performance* 5, 669–682.

Postle, B. R. (2005). Delay-period activity in the prefrontal cortex: One function is sensory gating. *Journal of Cognitive Neuroscience*, *17*(11), 1679–1690. https://doi.org/10.1162/089892905774589208

  (2006). Working memory as an emergent property of the mind and brain. *Neuroscience*, *139*(1), 23–38. https://doi.org/10.1016/j.neuroscience.2005.06.005

  (2015). Activation and Information in Working Memory Research. In *The Wiley Handbook on the Cognitive Neuroscience of Memory* (pp. 21–43). Wiley-Blackwell. https://doi.org/10.1002/9781118332634.ch2

Postle, B. R., Berger, J. S., & D'Esposito, M. (1999). Functional neuroanatomical double dissociation of mnemonic and executive control processes contributing to working memory performance. *Proceedings of the National Academy of Sciences*, *96*(22), 12959–12964. https://doi.org/10.1073/pnas.96.22.12959

Postle, B. R., & D'Esposito, M. (1999). "What" – then – "where" in visual working memory: An event-related fMRI study. *Journal of Cognitive Neuroscience*, *11*(6), 585–597. https://doi.org/10.1162/089892999563652

Postle, B. R., Druzgal, T. J., & D'Esposito, M. (2003). Seeking the neural substrates of visual working memory storage. *Cortex*, *39*(4), 927–946. https://doi.org/10.1016/S0010-9452(08)70871–2

Power, J. D., & Petersen, S. E. (2013). Control-related systems in the human brain. *Current Opinion in Neurobiology*, *23*(2), 223–228. https://doi.org/10.1016/j.conb.2012.12.009

Rademaker, R. L., Bloem, I. M., De Weerd, P., & Sack, A. T. (2015). The impact of interference on short-term memory for visual orientation. *Journal of Experimental Psychology. Human Perception and Performance*, *41*(6), 1650–1665. https://doi.org/10.1037/xhp0000110

Rademaker, R. L., Chunharas, C., & Serences, J. T. (2019). Coexisting representations of sensory and mnemonic information in human visual cortex. *Nature Neuroscience*, *22*(8), 1336–1344.

Ranganath, C., Johnson, M. K., & D'Esposito, M. (2000). Left anterior prefrontal activation increases with demands to recall specific perceptual information. *The Journal of Neuroscience: The Official Journal of the Society for Neuroscience*, *20*(22), RC108.

Ranganath, C., DeGutis, J., & D'Esposito, M. (2004). Category-specific modulation of inferior temporal activity during working memory encoding and maintenance. *Brain Research. Cognitive Brain Research*, *20*(1), 37–45. https://doi.org/10.1016/j.cogbrainres.2003.11.017

Reddy, L., Kanwisher, N. G., & VanRullen, R. (2009). Attention and biased competition in multi-voxel object representations. *Proceedings of the National Academy of Sciences*, *106*(50), 21447–21452. https://doi.org/10.1073/pnas.0907330106

Reynolds, J. H., & Chelazzi, L. (2004). Attentional modulation of visual processing. *Annual Review of Neuroscience*, *27*(1), 611–647. https://doi.org/10.1146/annurev.neuro.26.041002.131039

Riddle, J., Hwang, K., Cellier, D., Dhanani, S., & D'Esposito, M. (2019). Causal evidence for the role of neuronal oscillations in top–down and bottom–up attention. *Journal of Cognitive Neuroscience*, 31(5),768–779. https://doi.org/10.1162/jocn_a_01376

Riggall, A. C., & Postle, B. R. (2012). The relationship between working memory storage and elevated activity as measured with functional magnetic resonance imaging. *The Journal of Neuroscience*, *32*(38), 12990–12998. https://doi.org/10.1523/JNEUROSCI.1892–12.2012

Rigotti, M., Barak, O., Warden, M. R., Wang, X. J., Daw, N. D., Miller, E. K., & Fusi, S. (2013). The importance of mixed selectivity in complex cognitive tasks. *Nature*, *497*(7451), 585–590.

Riley, M. R., & Constantinidis, C. (2016). Role of prefrontal persistent activity in working memory. *Frontiers in systems neuroscience*, *9*, 181.

Rissman, J., Gazzaley, A., & D'Esposito, M. (2008). Dynamic adjustments in prefrontal, hippocampal, and inferior temporal interactions with increasing visual working memory load. *Cerebral Cortex*, *18*(7), 1618–1629. https://doi.org/10.1093/cercor/bhm195

(2009). The effect of non-visual working memory load on top-down modulation of visual processing. *Neuropsychologia*, *47*(7), 1637–1646. https://doi.org/10.1016/j.neuropsychologia.2009.01.036

Rose, N. S., LaRocque, J. J., Riggall, A. C., Gosseries, O., Starrett, M. J., Meyering, E. E., & Postle, B. R. (2016). Reactivation of latent working memories with transcranial magnetic stimulation. *Science*, *354*(6316), 1136–1139. https://doi.org/10.1126/science.aah7011

Rubinov, M., & Sporns, O. (2010). Complex network measures of brain connectivity: Uses and interpretations. *NeuroImage*, *52*(3), 1059–1069. https://doi.org/10.1016/j.neuroimage.2009.10.003

Saad, E., & Silvanto, J. (2013). how visual short-term memory maintenance modulates subsequent visual aftereffects. *Psychological Science*, *24*(5), 803–808. https://doi.org/10.1177/0956797612462140

Sadaghiani, S., Poline, J.-B., Kleinschmidt, A., & D'Esposito, M. (2015). Ongoing dynamics in large-scale functional connectivity predict perception. *Proceedings of the National Academy of Sciences of the United States of America*, *112*(27), 8463–8468. https://doi.org/10.1073/pnas.1420687112

Sauseng, P., Klimesch, W., Heise, K. F., Gruber, W. R., Holz, E., Karim, A. A., . . . Hummel, F. C. (2009). brain oscillatory substrates of visual short-term memory capacity. *Current Biology*, *19*(21), 1846–1852. https://doi.org/10.1016/j.cub.2009.08.062

Scimeca, J. M., Kiyonaga, A., & D'Esposito, M. (2018). Reaffirming the sensory recruitment account of working memory. *Trends in Cognitive Sciences*, *22*(3), 190–192. https://doi.org/10.1016/j.tics.2017.12.007

Serences, J. T. (2016). Neural mechanisms of information storage in visual short-term memory. *Vision Research*, *128*, 53–67. https://doi.org/10.1016/j.visres.2016.09.010

Serences, J. T., Ester, E. F., Vogel, E. K., & Awh, E. (2009). Stimulus-specific delay activity in human primary visual cortex. *Psychological Science*, *20*(2), 207–214. https://doi.org/10.1111/j.1467–9280.2009.02276.x

Sneve, M. H., Magnussen, S., Alnæs, D., Endestad, T., & D'Esposito, M. (2013). Top–down modulation from inferior frontal junction to FEFs and intraparietal sulcus during short-term memory for visual features. *Journal of Cognitive Neuroscience, 25*(11), 1944–1956. https://doi.org/10.1162/jocn_a_00426

Sneve, M. H., Sreenivasan, K. K., Alnæs, D., Endestad, T., & Magnussen, S. (2015). Short-term retention of visual information: Evidence in support of feature-based attention as an underlying mechanism. *Neuropsychologia, 66*, 1–9. https://doi.org/10.1016/j.neuropsychologia.2014.11.004

Soto, D., Greene, C. M., Kiyonaga, A., Rosenthal, C. R., & Egner, T. (2012). A parieto-medial temporal pathway for the strategic control over working memory biases in human visual attention. *The Journal of Neuroscience, 32* (49), 17563–17571. https://doi.org/10.1523/JNEUROSCI.2647–12.2012

Soto, D., Hodsoll, J., Rotshtein, P., & Humphreys, G. W. (2008). Automatic guidance of attention from working memory. *Trends in Cognitive Sciences, 12*(9),342–348.

Soto, D., Wriglesworth, A., Bahrami-Balani, A., & Humphreys, G. W. (2010). Working memory enhances visual perception: Evidence from signal detection analysis. *Journal of Experimental Psychology: Learning, Memory, and Cognition, 36*(2), 441.

Sprague, T. C., Adam, K. C., Foster, J. J., Rahmati, M., Sutterer, D. W., & Vo, V. A. (2018). Inverted encoding models assay population-level stimulus representations, not single-unit neural tuning. *Eneuro, 5*(3).

Sprague, T. C., Ester, E. F., & Serences, J. T. (2016). Restoring latent visual working memory representations in human cortex. *Neuron, 91*(3), 694–707. https://doi.org/10.1016/j.neuron.2016.07.006

Sprague, T. C., Saproo, S., & Serences, J. T. (2015). Visual attention mitigates information loss in small- and large-scale neural codes. *Trends in Cognitive Sciences, 19*(4), 215–226. https://doi.org/10.1016/j .tics.2015.02.005

Sreenivasan, K. K., Curtis, C. E., & D'Esposito, M. (2014). Revisiting the role of persistent neural activity during working memory. *Trends in Cognitive Sciences, 18*(2), 82–89. https://doi.org/10.1016/j.tics.2013.12.001

Sreenivasan, K. K., & D'Esposito, M. (2019). The what, where and how of delay activity. *Nature Reviews Neuroscience, 20*, 466–481. https://doi.org /10.1038/s41583-019–0176-7

Sreenivasan, K. K., Gratton, C., Vytlacil, J., & D'Esposito, M. (2014). Evidence for working memory storage operations in perceptual cortex. *Cognitive, Affective, & Behavioral Neuroscience, 14*(1), 117–128. https://doi.org/10 .3758/s13415-013–0246-7

Sreenivasan, K. K., & Jha, A. P. (2007). Selective attention supports working memory maintenance by modulating perceptual processing of distractors.

Journal of Cognitive Neuroscience, 19(1), 32–41. https://doi.org/10.1162/jocn.2007.19.1.32

Sreenivasan, K. K., Vytlacil, J., & D'Esposito, M. (2014). Distributed and dynamic storage of working memory stimulus information in extrastriate cortex. *Journal of Cognitive Neuroscience, 26*(5), 1141–1153. https://doi.org/10.1162/jocn_a_00556

Stokes, M. G. (2015). "Activity-silent" working memory in prefrontal cortex: A dynamic coding framework. *Trends in Cognitive Sciences, 19*(7), 394–405. https://doi.org/10.1016/j.tics.2015.05.004

Störmer, V. S., & Alvarez, G. A. (2014). Feature-based attention elicits surround suppression in feature space. *Current Biology, 24*(17), 1985–1988. https://doi.org/10.1016/j.cub.2014.07.030

Suzuki, M., & Gottlieb, J. (2013). Distinct neural mechanisms of distractor suppression in the frontal and parietal lobe. *Nature Neuroscience, 16*(1), 98–104. https://doi.org/10.1038/nn.3282

Teng, C., & Kravitz, D. J. (2019). Visual working memory directly alters perception. *Nature Human Behaviour, 3*(8), 827–836.

Theeuwes, J., Kramer, A. F., & Irwin, D. E. (2011). Attention on our mind: The role of spatial attention in visual working memory. *Acta Psychologica, 137*(2), 248–251.

Thompson-Schill, S. L., D'Esposito, M., Aguirre, G. K., & Farah, M. J. (1997). Role of left inferior prefrontal cortex in retrieval of semantic knowledge: A reevaluation. *Proceedings of the National Academy of Sciences, 94*(26), 14792–14797.

Thompson-Schill, S. L., D'Esposito, M., & Kan, I. P. (1999). Effects of repetition and competition on activity in left prefrontal cortex during word generation. *Neuron, 23*(3), 513–522. https://doi.org/10.1016/S0896-6273(00)80804-1

Thompson-Schill, S. L., Jonides, J., Marshuetz, C., Smith, E. E., D'Esposito, M., Kan, I. P., . . . Swick, D. (2002). Effects of frontal lobe damage on interference effects in working memory. *Cognitive, Affective, & Behavioral Neuroscience, 2*(2), 109–120. https://doi.org/10.3758/CABN.2.2.109

Tsotsos, J. K., Culhane, S. M., Kei Wai, W. Y., Lai, Y., Davis, N., & Nuflo, F. (1995). Modeling visual attention via selective tuning. *Artificial Intelligence, 78*(1–2), 507–545. https://doi.org/10.1016/0004-3702(95)00025-9

Umemoto, A., Drew, T., Ester, E. F., & Awh, E. (2010). A bilateral advantage for storage in visual working memory. *Cognition, 117*(1), 69–79. https://doi.org/10.1016/j.cognition.2010.07.001

van Kerkoerle, T., Self, M. W., & Roelfsema, P. R. (2017). Layer-specificity in the effects of attention and working memory on activity in primary visual cortex. *Nature Communications*, *8*, 13804. https://doi.org/10.1038/ncomms13804

van Moorselaar, D., Theeuwes, J., & Olivers, C. N. L. (2014). In competition for the attentional template: Can multiple items within visual working memory guide attention? *Journal of Experimental Psychology: Human Perception and Performance*, *40*(4), 1450–1464. https://doi.org/10.1037/a0036229

Voytek, B., Kayser, A. S., Badre, D., Fegen, D., Chang, E. F., Crone, N. E., . . . D'Esposito, M. (2015). Oscillatory dynamics coordinating human frontal networks in support of goal maintenance. *Nature Neuroscience*, *18*(9), 1318–1324. https://doi.org/10.1038/nn.4071

Watanabe, K., & Funahashi, S. (2015). Primate models of interference control. *Current Opinion in Behavioral Sciences*, *1*, 9–16. https://doi.org/10.1016/j.cobeha.2014.07.004

Wolff, M. J., Jochim, J., Akyürek, E. G., & Stokes, M. G. (2017). Dynamic hidden states underlying working-memory-guided behavior. *Nature Neuroscience*, *20*(6), 864–871. https://doi.org/10.1038/nn.4546

Woodman, G. F., & Luck, S. J. (2007). Do the contents of visual working memory automatically influence attentional selection during visual search? *Journal of Experimental Psychology: Human Perception and Performance*, *33*(2), 363.

   (2010). Why is information displaced from visual working memory during visual search? *Visual Cognition*, *18*(2), 275–295. https://doi.org/10.1080/13506280902734326

Wutz, A., Loonis, R., Roy, J. E., Donoghue, J. A., & Miller, E. K. (2018). Different levels of category abstraction by different dynamics in different prefrontal areas. *Neuron*, *97*(3), 716–726. https://doi.org/10.1016/j.neuron.2018.01.009

Xu, Y. (2017). Reevaluating the sensory account of visual working memory storage. *Trends in Cognitive Sciences*, *21*(10), 794–815. https://doi.org/10.1016/j.tics.2017.06.013

Yoon, J. H., Curtis, C. E., & D'Esposito, M. (2006). Differential effects of distraction during working memory on delay-period activity in the prefrontal cortex and the visual association cortex. *NeuroImage*, *29*(4), 1117–1126. https://doi.org/10.1016/j.neuroimage.2005.08.024

Yu, Q., Teng, C., & Postle, B. R. (2020). Different states of priority recruit different neural representations in visual working memory. *PLOS Biology, 18*(6), e3000769.

Yue, Q., Martin, R. C., Hamilton, A. C., & Rose, N. S. (2019). Non-perceptual regions in the left inferior parietal lobe support phonological short-term memory: Evidence for a buffer account? *Cerebral Cortex, 29*(4), 1398–1413. https://doi.org/10.1093/cercor/bhy037

Cambridge Elements ☰

Perception

James T. Enns
The University of British Columbia

Editor James T. Enns is Professor at the University of British Columbia, where he researches the interaction of perception, attention, emotion, and social factors. He has previously been Editor of the *Journal of Experimental Psychology: Human Perception and Performance* and an Associate Editor at *Psychological Science, Consciousness and Cognition, Attention Perception & Psychophysics,* and *Visual Cognition.*

Editorial Board

About the Series

The modern study of human perception includes event perception, bidirectional influences between perception and action, music, language, the integration of the senses, human action observation, and the important roles of emotion, motivation, and social factors. Each Element in the series combines authoritative literature reviews of foundational topics with forward-looking presentations of the recent developments on a given topic.

Cambridge Elements ⁼

Perception

Elements in the Series

Printed in the United States
By Bookmasters